Show Me the Way
to *Go Home*

SHIRLEY M. ODLE

Inspiring Voices®

A Service of **Guideposts**

Inspiring Voices books may be ordered through booksellers or by contacting:

Inspiring Voices
1663 Liberty Drive
Bloomington, IN 47403
www.inspiringvoices.com
1-(866) 697-5313

Because of the dynamic nature of the Internet, any web addresses or links contained in this book may have changed since publication and may no longer be valid. The views expressed in this work are solely those of the author and do not necessarily reflect the views of the publisher, and the publisher hereby disclaims any responsibility for them.

Any people depicted in stock imagery provided by Thinkstock are models, and such images are being used for illustrative purposes only.

Certain stock imagery © Thinkstock.

ISBN; 978-1-4624-0165-9 (sc)
ISBN; 978-1-4624-0164-2 (e)

Library of Congress Control Number: 2012939077

Printed in the United States of America

Inspiring Voices rev. date: 06/08/2012

hank you for opening my book of memories. I hope you will find this an interesting story, beginning in the roaring twenties and continuing into the present time. As you read my book, you will see what life was like for me when I was a child. How rich and cherished are the memories of a family who loved, protected and wanted for me only the best. We were just plain folks and happy even though we didn't have much. We lived our lives fully and on our journey the God who had a plan for our lives guided us. Join me as I recall this lifetime of precious memories that began as a simple life in 1922 and is presently in the mind-boggling time of advancements and achievements of today.

At the celebration of Christ Memorial Church's 100th anniversary in September 2009, I met Marge McRae and Joy Harrison, friends who are writers and teachers of the Word. They had both written their life stories, and they thought I should write mine. So to please both of them, and my girls, I begin my yarn.

> "For I know the plans I have for you, declares the Lord, plans to prosper you and not to harm you, plans to give you hope and a future. Then you will call upon me and come and pray to me, and I will listen to you. You will seek me and find me when you seek me with all your heart."
>
> Jeremiah 29:11

Chapter 1

I was born in Rainier Valley in the stately two-story home of William and Anna Cross the parents of my father, Bill.

My mother, Hazel and father, Bill had enjoyed a whirlwind romance when Hazel was just sixteen and Bill twenty. They met at a dance where Bill was playing his banjo with a small group of his high school friends. All evening they had eyes for no one but each other.

The first chance they had, they eloped on the inter-urban electric car from Seattle to Tacoma, a forty-five mile trip, in a speedy four hours. Arriving there they were married by the first minister who was available.

Home in Seattle late that night, Hazel didn't dare tell her folks what she had done. How many days she was able to keep this secret I don't know. Mother's oldest brother Al was protective of his sister. One night when Daddy was kissing mother good night under an umbrella, Al told Daddy to go home and leave his sister alone.

When the truth finally came out, my folks moved in with Daddy's parents. This was a great loss to the Abernathy family, as Hazel, the oldest daughter, was needed to watch the babies and help with household tasks in their Queen Anne Hill home.

Mother's family consisted of seven children: Al, Rollin, Hazel, Bess, Helen, Bob, and baby Virginia. Lydia was her mother, and Albert, her traveling salesman father. Without a car or any other means of transportation, Grandpa Albert Abernathy walked from house to house selling Singer sewing machines and various merchandise, such as coupons for pictures that would be taken by a photographer later at a prearranged time. Gone for days, no matter the weather, tramping on foot from farm to farm, he sold his wares. Many times he came home discouraged, with but a few dollars to buy the absolute necessities of life. Money was scarce and times were difficult in the 1920's, and compared to our present day of affluence, you would think they were really poor. Yet all nine of them were as happy as a large family could be on a salesman's unpredictable salary, and they made do with what they had.

Mother used to tell the story of how she had received from a sailor friend, a white middy blouse that she washed every night. Then early the next morning, her father ironed it so she'd have a clean blouse to wear to school each day.

My sister was born the first year of my parent's marriage and Daddy named her after a popular song entitled "Margie" that goes like this. "Margie, I'm always thinking of you Margie. I'll tell the world I love you, Don't forget your promise to me." Are you able to remember it?

Daddy worked for the Imperial Candy Company, and when we were kids he told all kinds of gruesome stories of how he had to sweep up the candy that fell to the floor and make licorice from it. That sure changed my desire to eat licorice.

Playing his banjo for dances wasn't enough to support a young family of three, so Daddy and Mother took Margie and headed to Eastern Oregon to mine for gold. Can you imagine such a scatter-brained decision to make, for a man and his wife with a newborn? But of course they were young, with big ideas, and they had to learn by experience just as we all did.

Settling southeast of Baker, Oregon in Durkee, a small railroad town in the mountains, they were befriended by the Engstroms, who owned a real working western ranch. The Engstroms let the little family live in a weather-beaten shack built by miners, in the crack between two merging sagebrush-covered hills. When he wasn't looking for gold, Daddy worked part-time as a signal engineer for the Union Pacific Railroad, which passed through their town.

It wasn't long before the excitement of prospecting wore off and reality set in. It was winter when they moved into that prospector's shack, and they were so cold, so very, very cold. Many new experiences took all the romance out of their adventure; such as seeing a snake slither up onto the window ledge where baby Margie was sleeping in her little bed, or being so hungry for food that Daddy had to swipe vegetables out of someone's garden to bring home for Mother to cook. Other simple luxuries such as a good meal were hard to come by, especially when their main course was potatoes baked with mashed turnips.

Daddy would get up on a coal car as the train slowly crawled up the grade and throw pieces of coal off to burn in their stove at home. It would be terrible when the train went through early in the morning, and being out of coal, Mother would have to hustle up enough coal until Daddy got home. I wonder if they found a nugget of gold or even some fool's gold for all their sacrifice?

Although the Engstroms had been good to the young couple and loved baby Margie like their own grandchild, Daddy and Mother made the decision to go home to Grandpa and Grandma Cross' place in Seattle to await the October, 1922 arrival of Daddy's "boy."

Back home, living with their folks didn't relieve them of their responsibility to contribute to the household cookie jar, so Daddy still had to find a job to support his growing family. He decided the new airplane industry would be an interesting place to work and eagerly went to the Boeing employment office to apply. The interviewer pointed out to Daddy that he hadn't graduated from Franklin High School, or even built a play airplane when he was a kid.. They gave him the only job they felt he had some experience doing, sweeping floors. In Boeing's old red barn he swept floors all day long from morning until night and that wasn't a very glamorous job. Almost everyone had the theory that planes couldn't fly anyway, and this business probably wouldn't really amount to much. So Daddy quit that job and decided the telephone company would be where he would next seek his fortune.

Mother made him a sack-lunch and he went to the phone company's employment office to apply. Surely, he would start work that day and would need a nourishing lunch. Much to his surprise, they told him he was not qualified for any existing job and should return home and wait for their call.

What he told Mother that night, only they could tell you, but I imagine it was a tall tale. Not knowing the truth, Mother continued to make his lunch daily and he went off "to work," visiting the telephone company employment office and sitting there from morning till night. Finally, after a week of seeing his expectant face in the waiting room, the interviewers decided to employ Daddy to get rid of him. Daddy was a smart man and took this job opportunity seriously. He fit right into the technology of the company and advanced quickly. It wasn't long before he was surprising those reluctant employment examiners by becoming a teacher to new employees in the rapidly growing phone company.

As days passed, the arrival of his hoped for "boy" was rapidly approaching, and one Friday night on October 13, 1922, I decided it was time to make my entrance into this strange new world. The Doctor was notified and it was decided that the delivery would take place right there, in Grandma's house. Mother's doctor, Dr. Theil, had a date that night and he picked up his girlfriend on the way to the dance and brought her with him to wait, while he delivered the baby. It was a good thing that Grandma had already delivered several babies, as I was already in this world testing my lung capacity before the doctor arrived.

When Mother first saw me she said, "That's not my baby, she looks like an Indian with black wild hair and a fat, round, red face." I weighed 10 pounds 6 ounces and was not a boy, as Daddy had wanted.

Grandma assured the new parents that I was a beautiful, healthy girl and they should be really proud of me. They named me Shirley, Mother's middle name, and Marion the middle name of her older brother Rollin. It was Friday the 13th and supposed to be a bad luck day. It was a good one for me though, as God placed me into the precious hands of such a loving family.

Daddy's work took the four of us to Oakland, California and we rented a home, with daddy commuting to San Francisco by ferry to teach phone company employees the new system Pacific Northwest Bell was installing. We lived in Oakland, near another young telephone family, Ed and Mable Lynch with their two daughters Lillian, my age, and Shirley Mae a couple of years younger than Lillian. We became close friends of the Lynch family. Lillian and I were in the same grade, played together and got into the same trouble.

The folks took Margie and me to the St. Stephens Methodist Episcopal Church and both of us girls received Christian baptism on the twenty-eighth day of March in 1926. Although I do not advise infant baptism, I am so glad they started Margie and me out right, by getting us established in a church. We both had no idea what was going on during the service, but the Lord did and He received us into His arms and loved and protected us both from that day on.

Though I don't remember each place, I was told we lived in three different houses in Oakland. The first place was close to a small business section of town where all the houses were separated by tall wooden fences. We walked on the top of these fences and visited our playmates by jumping down into their yards. If they were not in the yard, we would call out their names to get them to come out and play.

Neighbor kids would do the same at our house, until one day a playmate tried to climb into the back window of our house by standing on a rain barrel nestled against the house. The top broke and he fell in, hurting himself. All his crying alerted my folks and probably those next door. That ended our fence walking.

Marge and I went to Sunday School in that Episcopal Church near our house. My memories of a class are nonexistent, but I do remember a boy daring me to climb up after class to pull the fire alarm, and you know what I did. When I heard all the noise of the fire bells ringing I ran home as fast as I could. The first place of safety I thought of was under my bed, and that's where I headed. Daddy pretended he was a police officer looking for a bad little girl and he rang the front porch doorbell and came stomping into my bedroom, making a big fuss. Boy, was I afraid. I was sure the police were coming to get me. You couldn't get me near a fire alarm again. That was one of the very first important lessons I learned.

My first memories of school were Mother enrolling me in a preschool near our house. The first day of school, when it was naptime, I fell asleep and the teacher couldn't wake me up. So she let me sleep the rest of the afternoon. I probably wasn't doing much anyway, other than fighting over the crayons.

We had friends in the Seattle area, who raised English Bulldogs. They called my folks to tell them they had a batch of pups and wondered if we wanted one. Of course we jumped at the chance, and the Saxby's sent us two thoroughbreds. One for us, and the other for someone else in the area. The dogs were shipped in a large wooden crate with straw on the floor. The crate was clean when they arrived. However, when the express driver put the crate in Mother's laundry room and let the dogs out, the crate was still clean but the laundry room wasn't. We named our dog Dutchy. She was a darling dog with bright eyes and an ugly face. Beauty is truly in the eyes of the beholder. Her coat was white with black and brown spots. We loved her so and all the kids and their parents in the neighborhood loved her too.

Dutchy sat on a little chair that had a woven cane seat and we put that chair near the stove in the kitchen so she could keep warm. Sitting there, where she was so nice and comfy she would go to sleep and fall off her chair. She'd get up and climb on the chair again. She did this so often that she wore a hole in the seat. One day when we left the house, one of us girls left her doll on Dutchy's chair and when we got home that doll was torn to pieces. What right did that doll have to sit on her chair? Grandma LaDuke had sent us girls' two beautiful big dolls. Margie loved her doll and played with her, rocking her to sleep before carefully putting her in her cradle. Mother said I probably didn't care much for mine except to drag her around by one arm. I don't remember whose doll was destroyed on that chair, but Margie thought it was mine.

Our entertainment in those days was very limited. This of course was before TV, cell phones, electronic games or computers. We made our own entertainment. We had great fun playing board games, Authors, Checkers, Old Maid, and other card games that are still played today. Some games really got wild, as the loser chased the winner around the house and the fun turned into a knock down fight. A few people had pianos, string instruments, drums etc. and singing around the piano was in fashion for those who could afford one of these instruments.

Both Margie and I started taking piano lessons and I wasn't pleased about that, as it was too restrictive for me. I wanted to get outside where the action was and play with all the boys. I remember one time, Mother had given me quite an ultimatum regarding how much practice time I had to complete every day. I was so mad at Mother, I turned around and stuck my tongue out at her, only to see that she was looking back at me. What a shock to be caught. I never forgot the look on her face. I had actually hurt her feelings by my ungrateful actions. My folks had paid considerable money to get a piano and then gave us both lessons and I didn't even appreciate their sacrifice and the opportunity I was given.

Daddy was always tinkering with gadgets, and one day he brought home a kit to make a crystal radio set. It didn't take him long to put it together. A couple of round wire objects, with wires going from one side of the gadget to the other with no covering over it. You could see the innards. We had no idea what to expect from this contraption. But, when Daddy touched just the right wires together we heard squeaks and squawks. It wasn't long before some scratchy music was heard. Eureka, we had a radio. The trick of it was that you had to put your ear close enough to hear the music or the speaker. Can you imagine not having a radio blaring at the top of its capacity all day long? Or a TV, or tape recording, as we do today? Guess that's why Mother wanted us girls to be able to play the piano, so we could be the life of the party. Better than a drum, don't you think?

Our friends, the Lynches, lived next door to a Catholic church, that had a residence behind the church for the Sisters. One day, when Lillian and I were playing by the church, I found a sucker with tiny sugar ants on it and I picked it up not knowing what to do with it. I spied the Sisters' white lace habits, picked one out and threw the sticky candy at it. Right on target, the candy stuck. At the same time, the window opened and someone called out some words I was told not to remember. That's another place I didn't pass again. What on earth was I thinking? It must have been the influence I received from the bad boys in school, not the evil that was lurking in my own heart.

I started school in Burbank Elementary, at the age of five. The school was named after Luther Burbank, a famous horticulturist, who lived from 1849–1926 and produced a number of new plant varieties. I loved school. I was bright and outgoing and loved recess.

"Look out boys, here comes Shirley." I didn't care if my bangs were in my face or my socks falling down, all I wanted to do was play and play hard. That seems to have been my attitude all my life. When they wanted someone to do a stunt, they said, "Ask Shirley, she'll do it," and they weren't disappointed. I wasn't shy or afraid of people, which sometimes was good and at other times foolhardy. I got into some awful messes and of course, I had to follow through to save face.

The second house we lived in was several blocks from our original home and Grandma Abernathy and Aunt Virginia lived across the street from us, in a tiny little place about as big as a storage shed. Grandma also commuted to San Francisco, to work in the ferry terminal, in a place called "The Keys." This place was only a small counter where the daily newspaper or latest magazine, cigarettes, chewing gum, candy etc. were sold to those wanting items quickly, before getting on the ferry. She always said it was only temporary work, because some day her "ship would come in," and then she wouldn't have to work. I didn't quite know what she meant, but I kept looking for that ship to come sailing into San Francisco Bay.

Our house was next door to a Mexican couple, the Fernandes, who were loud and quarrelsome. Mother used to stand in our bathtub in the bathroom, and listen to their fights. We had only a small little window over the tub and Mother would stand on her tiptoes, to see if she could see some action. She really got a big kick out of doing that. I think that kind of activity is against the law now, isn't it?

Mother had a group of young women come over to our house regularly. They were probably about the same age as Mother, around 24 or 25. They met at our place to sew, talk and eat, while the kids played outside and looked for things to get into.

We had several different deliverymen who came up our street selling items that sparked our interest. One was Theo Creetis, the vegetable and fruit man. Another was the ragman, who drove a horse cart up our alley hollering "rags, anyone have rags." Probably the most interesting, was the iceman who delivered our ice. He chipped a large piece of ice into just the right size and carried it around on his back to put in the icebox on the back porch. When the ice melted, the water would drain down into a pan under the box. If it was your turn to empty the pan and you forgot, you had to answer to Daddy.

On the day of one of Mother's gatherings, all of us kids just happened to be watching the iceman do his delivery. When he left the ice cold, dripping truck, I crawled up into the back and grabbed several large chips of ice and hid them in my mouth so no one could see what I was doing. Running away excitedly, I accidentally swallowed the ice and blacked-out in the street. The kids screamed the alarm to their mothers and they all came running out, expecting the worse. When Mother saw it was me, she picked me up and got into a car parked by the curb, and started to honk the horn. Although the owner of the car didn't know Mother, he came running out of the house and drove Mother, with me on her lap, to the nearest doctor's office. I regained consciousness in the waiting room and wondered what all the commotion was. That was the last time I did that trick. I was starting to learn first hand some of the cold, hard lessons of life.

Most of the houses in our block had flat roofs, and the tops of the houses were covered with tar that had gravel in it. When the weather was hot, the tar melted and dripped down the drain spouts. We'd scoop up the tar and use it for black-jack gum. It was a little hard on our teeth though, with all that gravel in the tar. One good thing, we didn't have our permanent teeth in yet.

We made our last move to a house closer to Brighton Elementary, on the same street as Mills College. The house was on a hillside, with huge eucalyptus trees growing on top of the hill behind us, with tall, dry grass in a large field clear down to our house. All of us kids liked to play up there, hiding in the grass and then come cannon-balling down the hill to the back of our place.

I remember, we had to climb up cement steps to get to our house and on top by the landing we had a big butterfly bush, with beautiful purple flowers. Our house wasn't a mansion, but we had a million dollar view, at no charge.

The neighbors next door had a daughter who taught dancing lessons and Mother enrolled us. Margie did well, but I just couldn't seem to get those graceful steps. In place of artistic beauty, the teacher taught me comic dancing. In one recital, I was a Chinese boy with an umbrella. Mother made my costume and as I remember, my pajamas were bright orange and black. I had a black wig with a queue attached to it that hung down my back. Oh yes, I also wore a big smile all the time and jumped up and down all around on the stage. Somehow that smile became a permanent fixture and I've never gotten over it. My teacher tried to teach me to tap dance, but I could make only one foot do the right thing, so she gave up on me. What good was a one-footed, tap dancer? I don't know how proficient we really were as dancers but we had a great time dancing and I loved all the excitement. I was about six years old at the time and Daddy decided it was just another failed effort to get me in the theater.

There was a theater on the avenue, several blocks down the hill from our house and Mother let us go to the Saturday kids' matinee. I can't remember the shows, but I do remember all the screaming we did. One Saturday, they had kids come up on the stage. They asked them to dance or sing a song and you know who went up from our family. Margie was so mortified that she hid her head under her dress. She didn't want to look at me or even identify with me. I chose to dance the "Charleston," a kind of a fast dance, where you put your hands on your knees and switched your hands back and forth, while opening and shutting your legs. I thought I was an expert dancer, and probably would win one of the main prizes. The master of ceremonies held his hand over each of our heads after all the acts were finished, and the audience clapped to tell which one would win a prize. I didn't win the grand prize, but I did win a small five cent bag of potato chips that I ate before I got home. Did you know they had potato chips that long ago?

One Saturday, we asked Mother if we could go see the show, "The Gorilla" and she said "absolutely not." But we went anyway. I don't know where we got our nickel. We must have found it in the front room couch or a mason jar. When we got home, Daddy was waiting. I don't remember his spanking us, but I do remember Mother running with a stick in her hand around the couch in the living room, trying to catch me to give me a licking. While our dog barked at mother in all the excitement, Margie was yelling, "Shirley, stop and let Mama spank you, she'll catch you anyway." Her pleas didn't work and I don't remember the outcome of the discipline. However, I do remember the fear I had from seeing that show. There was a part where the actress puts her hand into the closet to get her fur coat, and she grabs the gorilla. After seeing that show, I was so afraid to go in my closet at night to get my nightgown that daddy had to give me a swat before I'd brave it. That was only after a lot of crying and stamping of feet. I remembered that fear for many, many years.

Mother found a potato bug in my bed one morning when she was making it and later told me about it. After that, I was really afraid whenever I got into bed that I would get my feet bit, so I slept with my body rolled up in a ball. Fear is a terrible thing. It can keep you safe and it can also keep you from doing the right thing.

In our front room, we had a small fireplace and Daddy would build a fire in the evening to warm up our house. There was a crack in the mantel and a couple of mice would put their tails through the crack to warm themselves. Daddy would gently pull on their tails and they would quickly yank their tails back into the crack. Fear could keep them from warming their tails but confidence would make them take a chance in order to get warm. That's true. You can ask my dad.

Mother got herself a job working part-time, in a small chocolate factory down on the avenue and she learned how to dip chocolates. The place where she worked also had a soda fountain up front that Margie and I frequented, if Mother would take us when she went to work. I don't remember another person working at the fountain, so I guess Mother helped us make our choice of treat. The chocolates that mother spoiled in the dipping process, she got to take home. I wonder how long it took Mother to figure out the reason why she had so many spoiled chocolates when she worked with us?

When we got home, we put the chocolates in small bags and went around to the neighbors selling them. The neighbors probably said, "Look, here comes those Cross girls, selling something again." We tried to sell California poppies too, but for some reason business was better for crushed and cracked chocolates than poppies. We hoped that Mother wouldn't get too good at dipping those chocolates, because perfect chocolates cut back on the saleable candy inventory. These first experiences of selling candy or poppies probably started my desire to make money. Once I got a job, I never got over the joy of spending the fruit of my labor. I was a lot like my grandmother Abernathy, she was looking for a job in the Want Ads until the day she passed away.

Chapter 2

Right at the peak of the 1929 depression, Daddy was transferred back to the Seattle office of the telephone company. He had just purchased a 1929 Ford sedan with wide running boards and a spare tire on the back. It was the latest mode of transportation and Daddy was proud of his first shiny new car. As the story is told Daddy paid $1000.00 cash for our car and Mother, Dutchy, Margie and I were to go ahead to Grandpa LaDukes' new chicken ranch and get settled there before Daddy reported back to work in Washington. For safety sake Mother advertised in the paper for a man to travel with us. The ad read, "Wanted, Brave Man to escort a woman with two girls and a dog in a new 1929 Ford touring car to Renton, Washington. Luggage space limited."

A homeless man answered mother's ad and she made arrangements for him to meet us. How strange he looked to a couple of little girls in his baggy clothes and all of his belongings wrapped in one small package of butcher paper. Before we got to Renton we found out he was a nice man without a job or family and on his own during the depression. He sat in the back seat between us girls and Dutchy, and we felt very safe with him there.

To travel from Oakland to Renton was a long trip and we stopped many times along the way to eat and stay in hotels. (Motels hadn't even been heard of in 1929.) Strangely whenever we stopped to eat the man would say he wasn't hungry and would watch our car with the dog and all our bags inside while we happily explored a new place to eat. After our meal Mother would bring back some toast or some other tidbit for the dog not even thinking of where the man was getting his food. At night the same process took place with him watching the car for us while we slept in the hotel. We didn't know when the man ate or even if he ate until one time I saw him sneak the food mother brought back for the dog. Blabbermouth squealed and all kinds of kids questions came pouring out of our mouths. He must of had no money other than what he gave mother for his trip to Washington. When we got to Seattle mother let him out on the side of the road and we never saw him again. This was typical of many wandering homeless men in 1929.

Well when we reached the chicken ranch everyone at grandma's house was almost as happy to see us as we were them. Climbing over belongings in complete disarray either inside or outside of the car we were happy to have reached our destination. I suppose grandma had a big celebration arranged for us when her first grandchildren arrived after that long, arduous drive home. Three cheers and a big kiss for Grandma and Grandpa LaDuke. Even our dog Dutchy's little stub tail was wagging as fast as it could go.

I think I should tell you some of grandma's story as the legacy she leaves is worth remembering. Anna Swan was born in Leksand, Sweden on October 19, 1876 to Olof and Christina Swan. I had been told that the Swans' had three girls Anna, Christy, Nettie and one boy Oscar. Nettie died as a young girl in her teens while they were still in Sweden and the rest of the family immigrated to the United States when Anna was seven years old.

The family lived on a farm near a river in Boone, Iowa from 1884-1886 and then traveled by wagon train to Yuma, Colorado where grandma grew up. She told stories of the hardships and dangerous experiences they endured as stoic Indians entered their home unbidden and sat staring at them. Not being able to communicate with them they had to sit there and wait for the Indians to make the first move.

Anna was twenty years old when she married William Cross in June 1896 in Denver, Colorado and they had three boys William who died at three months, Wilford who was called Bill and George. Daddy's father was a blacksmith and loved to play the piccolo. I saw this instrument and tried to play it when I was a small girl. My dad Bill was also a natural born musician playing the banjo by strumming it as a black man had taught him. (Usually you pick the banjo.) Grandpa Bill's banjo is displayed at our oldest girls' home in hopes that someone in the family would be inspired to play it as Daddy had.

The William Cross family moved to Seattle settling in the Rainier Valley area, which was at that time a dense forest of first growth timber. Daddy told of following his father when they walked all the way to downtown Seattle with Grandpa Cross playing his piccolo. Daddy said grandpa Cross told them he played as loudly as he could to scare the many black bears away. There were no roads then only trails through the forest and it was a long scary, but well marked trip to the waterfront. Loggers cut the tall first growth trees surrounding the main streets of Seattle and used the steep wet hills to skid their cut trees down to Puget Sound and on to the log mills to be rough cut into lumber. That slippery trick of getting the trees down a steep hill was called a "Skid Row" as it still is today.

When I was in college Grandma Abernathy and Aunt Virginia had an apartment on Yesler Way in the area at the top of that steep hill and cable cars like the ones in San Francisco were put in so people could get down quickly into the business district of Seattle. In some places the hill was so steep you had to hang on with all your strength to keep from falling out of that open trolley. No seat belts were provided or even heard of then. Aunt Virginia probably rode this trolley to where she worked in a little shop making and selling doughnuts at Putt's Doughnuts in the famous Pike Place Market.

Grandpa William Cross built the house I was born in there in the woods in Rainier Valley. He was a short thin, sick man much of his life and they lived in that big home until he passed away. Grandma then married her neighbor a young bachelor Ed LaDuke, who was a jack of all-trades. He had been a sea captain before he started building small homes in the Rainier Valley area and he made his living by renting and selling these small rough dwellings. We all lived in grandma's house together until after the depression and the government foreclosed on Grandpa LaDuke's rental houses and took away most of his income.

15

Grandpa LaDuke bought property on the Benson Highway south of Renton and as soon as his brother Mike came to live with them they built a lovely home and started to raise chickens.

Grandma LaDuke was a short, heavy woman. She had a wonderful disposition and when she laughed her whole body shook and you couldn't do anything but laugh too. She was everyone's friend and it wasn't unusual to have guests for dinner and visiting family members who stayed for extended periods of time. I remember sitting on her lap and listening to her exciting stories about travelers and her thoughts of what would happen in the future when they finally figured out how to travel in the sky. She was way ahead of her time when she would tell me that someday people would go up in the sky in some kind of a vehicle and wait for the world to turn around and then they'd land in a spot many miles away. I really believed these stories and believe it or not she wasn't far from the truth.

It was so much fun living with the LaDukes as there was always something going on. Once grandma had an afternoon dress up affair and mother bought Margie and me our first long dresses on sale from J. C. Penney's. It was our happy assignment to greet the guests and we went around shaking hands and trying to make everyone feel welcome.

Christmas was wonderful in their home too and people came from all over to be entertained. Grandma LaDuke didn't do a lot of decorating but they did have a nice tree that probably one of Santa's elves hand decorated. Santa even made his appearance all dressed up in a red suit and ringing bells accompanied by his deep bass voice. But Oh, the large oval table in the dining room was a sight to behold. A white linen table cloth was ringed in cut green boughs and every square inch of space on that large table was filled with delightful treats. To top it all off the large centerpiece was a Christmas goose whose juices and fragrance caused our taste buds to tingle.

This was a very special Christmas for all of us as we were celebrating the arrival of grandma's sweet little Patricia Jane who was chosen to be a new member of our family. How could we be so blessed to welcome both the Christ Child and Patricia Jane on that blessed night.

In the summer Grandma had her Scandinavian relatives and friends come on Sunday afternoons for big picnics under the bing cherry trees that grew along the front lawn of the house. She cooked a wonderful meal for her guests and after every morsel was devoured, Margie and I performed. In one of our short skits we dressed like sailors and sang a sailor's ditty. Wearing sailor hats and Margie down on one knee and me acting coy to his proposal, here is the song we sang.

"I'm just a sailor from across the seas,
Come to ask if you'll marry me.
Will you marry, marry, marry, marry me,
Will you marry, marry, me."

"Yes I'm just a sailor from across the seas,
Come to ask if you'll marry me.
Will you marry, marry, marry, marry me,
Will you marry, marry, me."

Grandma thought we were the greatest team since "little Orphan Annie and Sandy". Every place we went with them we had to perform that ditty or something else she provided.

The Scandinavians brought their instruments and they'd play the old hymns. Neighbors, who wondered what in the world was going on, would drift over and join in the singing. Everyone was always welcome at Grandma's house. Her gift of hospitality was passed on to my dad and other fortunate members of our family.

Grandma and Grandpa LaDuke's chicken farm was five or six miles south of Renton and besides the LaDukes and Uncle Mike our family lived there too. The house had three bedrooms upstairs, some vacant store rooms and an unfinished bathroom with running water but no toilet, just a hole in the floor where someday the toilet would be. The whole upstairs was where our family stayed when we came from California and we had the run of the house up and down three flights of stairs. In the middle of the surrounding third floor bedrooms was what they called a "sitting room" with a Victrola that had to be wound up to make it play. Those old songs we played were going almost night and day and I wonder how Grandpa and Grandma LaDuke stood it. French doors opened out on an over-hanging front deck where lovers such as Uncle George and his girlfriend Helen whispered in the dark.

This was a big farm with thousands and thousands of chickens. They got the chicks from the Washington Farmer's Association, and culled out for eating the few fryers they were sent by mistake and kept the pullets for the production of eggs. What a wonderful place for kids to be raised. Large long chicken houses that looked like army barracks were filled to capacity with darling little yellow chicks protected under big round-heated metal circular covers that were several feet off the floor. Under it they had the chicken mash and water in troughs and the chicks walked over and in them and made messes all over the floor. Chickens, chickens, chickens everyplace. It wasn't long before those cute little chicks were ugly dumb chickens raised solely for their eggs.

You might think that we ate a lot of chicken. Yep. We had it every way imaginable and I don't remember getting tired of it. A heaping plate of eggs that had been fried in genuine bacon grease in a black iron skillet were served every morning with a stack of homemade toast. You were expected to not just eat one egg but several. I remember Uncle Mike reaching clear across the table to spear four or five pieces of toast to eat with his bacon and eggs. Grandma was a great cook which the men's ample tummies substantiated.

Whenever we had a family in my grade at school who were down on their luck, Grandma sent a basket of canned goodies which included a nice dressed chicken, covered over with a dishcloth. All she wanted them to return was the basket so she could repeat the gift for someone else. Everyone thought I was from a rich home. I was, but not in money.

In the basement of the house they had a cool-room where hundreds of eggs a day were cleaned and put in large crates for the Washington Farmer truck to pick up. If you were not involved in something upstairs in the house you went down to the cool-room and cleaned eggs. We used a rough piece of fine sand-paper and lightly rubbed all the chicken debris off the eggs and packed them in the Washington Farmer crates. Grandpa gave the truck driver the eggs and he gave them mash for the chickens to eat with only a small amount of money exchanged.

Milk was also separated in this cool-room and we used the cream and milk in the kitchen and what was left over we would slop the pigs. Wow, did they squeal when they saw us coming with the sour cream. Grandpa LaDuke made a homemade elevator that originated in the cool-room and was pulled up by a rope into their large kitchen that held butter, milk, cream and things we would now put on our refrigerator shelves. This was not only an apparatus of convenience but also a great place to hide, although a bit dangerous. I remember sharing this hiding place with miscellaneous kitchen items as I cleverly hid from Margie.

Grandpa LaDuke also raised a steer every year for beef and a pig for bacon. When it was time to slaughter the animals a butcher came and handled the gory deed. I hated to hear the pig squeal but even worse the look in the eyes of that trusting steer was almost all I could tolerate. Grandma had a full basement that had a coal burning stove in the kitchen area where she had her large copper boiler going full blast most of the time for canning meat, vegetables and fruit.

There were times when everyone who was able to scrape a carrot or peel an apple was given a job and we had as many as five or six women working together to put up all those quarts of food for winter consumption. We had a blast and you might say it was a real party. Margie sometimes would complain that I purposely scraped carrot peelings in her face. Why, I would never think of such a trick.

Grandpa LaDuke had a large barn where he parked his car and a little Ford truck that he used in harvesting the sour cherry crop. I learned to drive a vehicle in that little truck, shifting a stick shift and working the clutch at the same time. In the barn in back of the shop there was a place where our Jersey cow was milked both morning and night. I couldn't figure out how she knew when to come in to be milked.

Of course when you have a barn you have plenty of hay and boy did we love that hay. We jumped in it and climbed up in the little cupola on the top of the barn and looked out over the landscape. We could see all kinds of things and no one could see us. It was real secretive like. Of course whenever you have hay you also have cats and with cats come lots of kittens. FREE. We always had a batch to play with. I remember one time grandma's little fox terrier Trixie had a batch of pups up there in the hay and before they had their eyes open Uncle George cut off their tails. They didn't even cry. Poor little things. I couldn't figure out why Uncle George cut off their tails because now they couldn't wag them to show how happy they were.

Grandpa's property was sloping west and just as you reached flat land there was a lovely little stream that bubbled around fallen moss covered logs and over rocks. I loved to go down there by myself and find an old sawed off tree that had a large enough stump for me to lie down on. I would look up in the sky and dream about the future and the grand things I would someday do. Would I be a movie actress, teacher, or a secretary who traveled the world? I chose the latter and even when I entered college I had that dream and took business administration classes so that some day I could make my fantasy come true.

We were well taken care of on that productive farm and we didn't want for anything. You wouldn't know we were in the middle of a depression and that there were many people who were desperate to find help.

Even children were expected to contribute to the family finances. Some kids in town had paper routes, mowed lawns, shined shoes, and worked for a neighboring farmer all day for a buck and a wholesome lunch prepared by his wife. They sold magazine subscriptions, delivered groceries and when they got home at night emptied the contents of their pockets on the kitchen table and all their earnings were added to the household money.

To be on welfare was not an option for most people we knew, as to receive money and not to have worked for it was shameful. So some rented out rooms in their homes for a small amount to help both the homeless and themselves. If you could sew you took in items for alterations. Whatever you could do you found a way to make yourself financially productive.

When Franklin Delano Roosevelt entered the Presidency, joblessness was close to 30% and he launched the CCC, Civilian Conservation Corps. Young workers in the program were given shelter, food, clothing and medical attention plus $1.00 a day in wages. For this they cleared brush, planted trees, fixed roads and developed state and national parks.

The name of the program was changed to "work relief" and a person received $10.00 a week in grocery and rent vouchers and participants were asked to work on public projects for enough hours to earn the $10.00.

I remember the chain letter dream of making money for very little effort and hardly any funds. We just made a copy of the letter with our name at the bottom and sent a dollar bill to the name on top of the letter and in a month or less you hoped to receive a dollar from everyone on the list. We tried them all and they always failed. There is nothing like a full days work for making money.

Daddy took us into downtown Seattle to see an emerging small town where homeless men were building shacks out of cardboard boxes, pieces of wood or scrap metal, whatever they could find. Everyone called it "Hoover Ville" named for President Herbert Hoover who many blamed for the economic conditions of the time. People came from all over the country riding freight train box cars to Seattle looking for hope and work and it wasn't unusual for a man to come to your backdoor asking for a job, a place to stay or something to eat. At our place they were hardly ever turned away.

There was a slogan everyone seemed to be chanting, "Go West young man, Go West." We were as far West as they could go without getting in the Pacific and the area was filled with young folks trying to make their fortune. If there was something they could do they were put to work and then given lodging and food as pay. There wasn't much money exchanged in those days and the barter system was the norm. Daddy's job at the telephone company was firm and he never missed a day's work. But he did miss pay for some of the days he worked. If you had a job you were happy to forfeit part of your salary because you could still provide for your family on a reduced paycheck.

Chapter 3

Margie and I started school in Henry Ford Elementary just inside the city limits of Renton. I had been in grade 3 1/2 in California and when I entered Henry Ford they didn't have the half grade system, so I was put in grade four. It was a large school and instead of Spanish Americans, we had Italian Americans and a few Scandinavians. The only difference between the kids in California and Washington was the color of their hair and skin. However the Italians had garlic breath and if you had someone in the desk behind you who had garlic for breakfast you knew they were there even before you saw them.

We didn't know the difference between the races in those days. We just had a great time playing with everyone and kicking up the dust on the playground or stomping our feet and singing loudly in assemblies. We went to school there in Renton until summer vacation and then Daddy decided we should get back on our own and move to Seattle in a little house behind his folks' big house where I had been born. Grandpa LaDuke had improved this little place and built an addition on the front where he put a bedroom and enlarged the front room. He also added a garage and fixed up the yard.

I loved this little place as the bedroom that was built on the front of the house was Margie's and my room. Where ever we went we shared our space which was a good lesson for siblings to learn. To love and respect each other was what brought us together as sisters and brothers and established a bond that was hard to break.

The new windows that Grandpa put across the west side of our house opened out toward the front of the property and we would sit in the windows and smell the flowers that Mother put in the flower boxes. Meanwhile we watched the boys do tricks on their bikes to try to impress us, as we were the new girls on the block.

Both of us girls were given piano lessons again. Our teacher was a little German man who traveled by bus to our house to give us our lessons. How I hated to see him come walking down the block with his little satchel in his hand. He was gruff and would slap my hands if I made a mistake or didn't respond to his directions.

When he got tired of coming to our house he asked mother to have us ride the city bus to his studio in downtown Seattle for our lessons. To go to school on the city bus it was five cents. Just to ride on the bus to town it was ten cents. The bus driver said we weren't going to school that late in the day and should pay full fare. So when we got on the bus Margie always got on first and made me put the money in the collection box for both of us. I had to argue with the driver that we were indeed going to school. Piano school that was. When the day for our lessons approached I dreaded looking that bus driver in the face. Those experiences were good for me though as I learned to face adversity and do the hard thing if it was necessary.

After our lesson we would go to the drug store soda fountain across the street from the teacher's studio and next to the telephone building where daddy was working. He said we could put a treat on his bill if we had a good lesson and we always said we had a good lesson. At the drug store, I got a pineapple milk shake and that treat was an incentive for me to work harder.

Margie learned to play the piano much better than I, as she put her heart into it and continued to work to be an accomplished pianist rather than just to get a treat. At home, when I practiced, I had an alarm clock on the end of the piano keys and kept watching the clock. As soon as my practice time was over, even if I was in the middle of a page, I headed out to play.

There was a big Bing cherry tree in the back yard of our house in Seattle that was my new dream tree. All alone, I would climb up that tree and talk to the Lord and myself and plan my future. I was now leaning toward being a movie actress and saw myself as beautiful and talented. I hoped when the time came they wouldn't ask me to dance, as my one foot still wouldn't do what it was supposed to do.

It was when we lived in this house that we were all changed spiritually. You see when Daddy got back to the phone company from California he met an old friend named Fitzmaurice. He had been quite a party guy and according to Daddy, used foul language on the job.

His wife, who was chronically ill and bedridden, and Fitzmaurice had an adult son who played the piano professionally. Their son played at major events in many churches and at camp meeting in Centralia, where we went every summer after we became Christians. Daddy first noticed the change in Fitzmaurice's speech and that he didn't smell of booze as he had previously. Mr. Fitzmaurice asked Daddy to go to church with him to hear brother and sister evangelists who were holding services in Georgetown Presbyterian Church. This was certainly a change and Daddy went along out of curiosity and came home a completely different person.

After that night, he was so happy he wanted us all to go the next night and hear those vibrant young people. We did and we all experienced the changing power of the gospel of Christ. I was only about seven at the time and Margie was nine. When I knelt at the altar I felt an overwhelming sensation of love and I knew I was a changed person and I wanted everyone to experience this joy. Don and Charlotte McCrossen explained to us, everyone has sinned and come short of God's perfection. Jesus was sent to earth to show us the way to become reconciled to the Father, "For God so loved the world that He sent His only Son that whosoever believeth in Him might not perish but have eternal life." John 3:16.

My decision to become a Christian was a lifetime commitment. Not that I was perfect, but that I was a cleansed child of God, and a member of His family.

What a change in our household. We had absolutely no fighting in our family. Ha, what a laugh. We were still humans and traveling this road with other travelers to the Kingdom who were just like us and needing daily contact with the Father. But, Daddy was now reading his Bible while sitting in a chair by the kitchen stove with an entirely different attitude. One big thing that really changed is that Daddy didn't smoke any more. After smoking for most of his life, God delivered him from cigarettes in one night. He took his cigarettes out of his pocket and laid them on the altar never to pick them up again. He had never been a drinker either, but there were times when he didn't come home at night because he would go to the show or some other place with his male friends. Now family and home and reading God's Word were most important to him and he was growing as a Christian each day.

Daddy started to go to Hollywood Temple in North Seattle with Mr. Fitzmaurice to a Bible study on prophecy and the end times. In fact he even took the minister of the church where we attended to go with him to this study. Then Daddy was asked to teach a college age men's class in our church and he had an artist make a large illustration of the dispensations of the Bible and Daddy put it up on the wall in his Sunday School room. When the board of the church heard of this they decided Daddy should not teach Sunday School there anymore.

From that time on we started attending Hollywood Temple regularly and our entire family drove clear up to the north-end of Seattle to attend. Margie and I were baptized together there in the baptismal tank in front of the church and that was one of our next public steps in our spiritual journey. We both had been baptized as children in California by the will of our folks, however this time we choose to be immersed in the baptismal tank to show we had given our lives to Christ and were now going to live our lives for Him.

We attended church on Sunday regularly, morning and night. They had a great orchestra in the evening service and so many young people were a part of this service. We made many lasting friends in that church and wherever we went we met many new members of God's family. The music was wonderful and our family was so happy to worship there. I loved the evening services, and I would stand up on my pew seat and say the same scripture every time I could, "Verily, verily, I say unto you, except a man be born again, he cannot see the kingdom of God."

John 3:3. Speaking out the Word of God was another step I took in my decision to follow the Savior.

In the fall, Margie and I were enrolled in Brighton Elementary School, the same school that Daddy had attended as a boy. It was an old three-story, gray school quite a distance from our home. I have vivid memories of the smell of apple sauce from a class where girls learned to cook, and the assemblies with everyone standing and reciting the pledge of allegiance to the flag of the United States, and on special days veterans of World War I, told us about war, and the pain many suffered because of it.

We spent days rehearsing our dance around the maypole and how to weave the colored ribbons to perfection. I had an elderly teacher who would push a small piano into our room and we would sing all the old songs such as Santa Lucia, America, Row, Row, Row Your Boat and many more. This teacher was tall and skinny and wore a wig. When she played the piano the naughty boys would go behind her and pretend to pick something out of her wig. If she happened to strike a wrong note on the piano she would then declare that the music was written that way and it was wrong. What vivid memories I have of Brighton Elementary School.

One day as Margie was walking home from school, she noticed a terrible fight in progress just across the street from the schoolyard. Two kids were going at it with all their might and she thought it looked like someone she knew. Could it really be a girl and boy fighting?. That just never happens. Margie ran as fast as she could to be sure it was who she thought it was. Yes, of all things it was her sister Shirley, swinging away wildly.

Margie broke up the fight and marched me right home. Here I was a new Christian and acting like that. My heart had been changed, but I still had a long way to go before my actions followed my heart. I'm so glad that my salvation does not depend on what I do, but on what Christ has done for me in paying the price for my sin. To this day, I don't know what the fight was about. It was the first and last time I ever used my fists to fight with anyone, but unfortunately, I sure have used my tongue. If I ever see that kid again I'll ask him why we were fighting and apologize for my part in it.

It was about this time that Bob, my mother's youngest brother, came with his friend Leo to live with us and work in Grandpa LaDuke's gas station on Rainier Avenue. Where in the world did we all sleep in that little house? I know we had only two bedrooms and there were a total of six of us.

Bob Abernathy was a happy young man, who loved to sing and was a lot of fun. As usual, when it was Sunday, we piled everyone into the Ford and took them to church. Daddy was like that wherever we went. He would assure Mother he could get everyone into the car and then he'd get in and tell everyone to pile in too. And somehow he got record numbers of kids in the back seat. The first time Bob attended church with us he accepted the Lord. He was so happy and would say silly things like, "I wonder if they will have spaghetti in heaven?"

Both Bob and Leo worked in Grandpa LaDuke's gas station together. Then Bob had a terrible accident. He was working in the garage and wanted to look down in a can to see if it had oil in it. He used a match instead of the flashlight he carried in his back pocket to see, and accidentally dropped the match into a wide pan with oil and it started to burn. Picking it up to carry it outside the garage, he slipped on grease and dumped the flaming oil down the front of his pants. With his pants on fire, he started to run and was tackled by someone who rolled him in the grass, only it was too late to keep him from being seriously burned. He was transported to Harborview Hospital in Seattle and they did everything known to do in 1932 for burns. After three months of excruciating pain he died.

I remember his terribly burned legs and the pain he suffered. He said over and over, "Why did I use that match when I had a flashlight in my back pocket?" Life is like that. Its a series of choices, and after we have made the choice we cannot undo it. His girlfriend Lyla came from California and was by his side everyday. A beautiful person, she faithfully stayed right with him until the Lord mercifully took him home.

It was then that Mother became pregnant again. The ladies of the Hollywood Church had a baby shower for her even though we were new in their church. They supported my mom in this pregnancy, as she was having a very difficult time over the loss of her brother and the heart trouble she had most of her life. Our brother Bobby was born on August 16, 1933 and Daddy had his boy at last. He was named after mother's brother and our Daddy, Robert Wilford Cross.

Daddy hired a farm girl from up in Big Lake near Mount Vernon, Washington who Heck and Sidney Lindbloom recommended and she came to live with us to help mother. Mother gave her directions from her bed where she spent a lot of time and the directions were carried out only when the girl decided she wanted to do it.

It turned out that the girl was pregnant too, and had to be sent home. We got another girl who was almost as bad as the first one who had to be instructed how to do everything. She was a large girl and really could pack away the food. In the morning she would use all the cream on her cereal before the family got up and Daddy wouldn't have cream for his coffee.

I suppose you wonder how come everyone had milk and cream during the depression? Well, almost everyone had a pet cow and the folks would stake "Daisy" out in the yard someplace and the kids were responsible for moving her when she had eaten all the grass in the original spot. We didn't have a cow but Grandma Cross had one when they lived in the big house where I was born.

I don't think our hired girl had ever ironed before she came to our place, as when she tried to iron out the wrinkles in Mother's seersucker dresses she had no success. She also used the same cleaning rags she cleaned up the toilet with to wash the floor. On her day off when her boyfriend was coming to pick her up, she surprised us at how fast she could work to be ready to go with him.

Bobby was such a darling baby. Margie and I both helped Mother with him. I remember one time when the folks went somewhere, she instructed us to give him a bottle when he got hungry. We hadn't made the formula before so we put the powdered milk in the bottle and added the water, shook it up and proceeded to feed him. He just nursed a little and then kicked his feet and giggled at us. We worked and worked to get that bottle of thick goo down him and we were finally successful. When Mother came home we found out we had used up all the powdered milk meant for that day. Mother was beside herself. She called the doctor and he laughed and said just give him water the rest of the day. We were relieved, as we were sure we'd done something life threatening to our darling baby brother.

Bobby didn't lack for attention. We gave him all of ours. He had a little scooter that he pushed around the front yard and one day it fell over with Bobby on it and his shoulder hit a stepping-stone in the lawn. He screamed and cried and we couldn't get him to stop. When Mother took him to the doctor he said he had broken his collar bone and there wasn't much he could do for him except tape it up and wait for it to heal. Now that's a switch. Today they would have him in for therapy immediately and a pill every other hour.

Chapter 4

A visit from Daddy's brother George and his wife Helen changed our lives again. They lived at Panther Lake, south of Renton and had planned to build their dream home on the lake's shore. To save money they planned to build the garage first and live in it while they were in the process of building their home.

Uncle George had just found that Helen had tuberculosis and must be hospitalized for a period of time with isolation and complete bed rest. The only place to treat her was in Firlands Sanitarium in North Seattle and you had to live within the city limits of Seattle to qualify for treatment. George and Helen couldn't afford to keep building their garage and rent in Seattle too. So Daddy and Mother offered to change houses with them to help Helen qualify. The house swap happened so fast that before we knew it we went from a house that was comfortable, to one with almost no conveniences except a sink on the main floor in the large main room.

Daddy and Mother's bedroom was behind the wall area where cars eventually would park and there were stairs from their bedroom leading up to a large unfinished second story room. Daddy put our dresser and bed in the unfinished second floor for Margie and me to use as a room for our bedroom. At night when we turned off the light it was pitch black. I was scared to death. I don't know what I'd have done without Margie. Did I say the garage was located in an area of fir trees and if we had to go to the bathroom during the night we had to go outside to the port-o-potty. Uncle George had also built the outhouse just outside the kitchen window and the toilet was the view we enjoyed when we looked toward Panther Lake. I definitely think we got the short end of the bargain. But we were doing the Christian thing to help them out and hopefully they would appreciate it.

There were some benefits though from the move. Daddy liked the fact that the area for his new telephone office was in Renton and our Grandpa and Grandma LaDuke would live probably a mile from us. Daddy started to look for acreage close by and found ten acres with a beautiful view of Panther Lake with Mt. Rainier in the background. I don't know how many pictures were taken with that view in mind. The property had one lone beautiful large fir tree and an old house that leaned over from the weight of the ivy growing all over it. When you walked in the old house you felt like you were in a spook house at the fair.

And yes, I forgot to mention there were several huge, beautiful pear and apple trees on the property. We enjoyed the fruit from these trees year after year. An old man had owned the property and Daddy was fortunate to be able to buy it from him and make plans to build the folks dream home there.

When Daddy finally found the type of home he wanted to build on those ten acres, he paid Grandpa LaDuke and his brother Mike, to do the job. Daddy acted as his own contractor, with help from various builders and sub-contractors, and our lovely English Tudor home was soon in the process of being built.

The brick for the house came from a demolished school and was a deep red color brick that was usually seen on Tudor homes. Slate covered the sharp, tall roof. The interior floors were hardwood, except the kitchen and laundry, which were linoleum, and the bathrooms were a lovely tile. The trim on the doors, windows and the baseboards were all mahogany.

Our front door entered into a sunroom along the front of the house and Daddy had bookcases built under the windows surrounding two sides of the room. We had a large front room, which we used for gatherings, prayer meetings and Bible studies. On the main floor we also had a dining room, beautiful kitchen, bathroom, laundry and the folk's bedroom. The second floor had three bedrooms with a small bath. A full basement had the usual cool room, sink area, with a large old-fashioned stove. When the house was finished it was lovely.

At this time Daddy was asked by a young Salvation Army man, Mr. Eric Johnson to consider taking over a little Sunday School he started in the Spring Glen area. The Sunday School on Renton School District property was in an old school house that the young man paid $1.00 a year to rent.

Part of the bargain was for Mr. Johnson to keep the building up. Mr. Johnson built a small kitchen off the side of the schoolhouse and put a sink for water along with tables and benches for more classes there. In the main room there was a potbelly stove and a number of benches for seating. Someone had donated an upright piano and a curtain was installed to separate the main room for several classes.

Daddy felt that this was an opportunity for our family to serve in the community so we took over the Spring Glen Sunday School and Daddy served there for 24 years. Most of the people who attended would not have had Sunday School or Church services there to attend if the folks hadn't taken it on. At first Margie played the piano, I led the singing and Daddy gave a chalk talk, which was a short illustrated Bible message. It was a thriving Sunday School and we were blessed with good teachers and fine Christian families from the area.

The talk in the neighborhood wasn't all positive though, as Daddy was told that some people thought we built our home with the children's offerings. What a laugh. We might have had a few dollar bills each Sunday in the offering from some of the adults, but usually the little kids brought only a little change. For the entire improvements Daddy did and supplies purchased he didn't come anywhere near the cost for our home. The folks really were giving so much of their time and money for the Sunday School because they loved the Lord and wanted to serve Him in this way.

Mr. Johnson started the Sunday School in 1934, and the first church services were held January 5, 1951 with Harris Lorenson a Renton Safeway worker as the part-time preacher. What a dedicated young man Harris was. It didn't take much for him to be overcome by the message he was presenting and have tears rolling down his cheeks.

The first service was not a formal service, just mostly praise, prayer, singing and getting acquainted. A board of trustees was appointed and Daddy suggested the name, Village Chapel. It wasn't until 1955 that this choice piece of property could be purchased from the school district for $2500.00.

Money to build a new church came in miraculously and when material was ordered the money was always available to pay for it. Volunteer crews of men from the church under the leadership of Grandpa LaDuke were the unpaid workers, and the women of the church made a full lunch for them every day they worked on the church. We began worshiping in the basement of the new church on October 5, 1952. The congregation grew so rapidly that some of the congregation returned to the old school building for classes until the new building was completed.

In May 1953, Harris Lorenson gave up his job at Safeway and became the full time pastor for $75.00 a week. Daddy continued as Sunday School Superintendent all without compensation until 1958 when he retired from the telephone company. The Village Chapel still continues to meet the spiritual needs of the people in the Spring Glen area under a new name and leadership.

When Uncle Stew Bereiter passed away in Portland, Aunt Bess and her two little girls moved in with the Crosses until she decided what to do. One Sunday morning Daddy was driving a carload of kids to Sunday school and I was sitting in the back seat with Janice, Sally and some other kids. Janice was holding on to the door handle and she opened the door and fell out of the car, rolling over and over with her black and red lined cloak flying in the wind. By the time Daddy got the car stopped, Janice was up and running to the car. We were going an average speed and only God could have kept her from being seriously injured. Can you imagine, she didn't have a scratch on her?

The kids in the neighborhood loved to play tricks on the Sunday School. One Sunday morning after Halloween, when Daddy came early to start the fire in the stove, he found most of the benches on the peaked roof of the building. He had to crawl up the steep, frosty roof and get them down. What a chore so early in the morning. He was a good sport about it and got a kick out of their ingenuity. Daddy probably played a few tricks on some buildings in his heyday on Halloween too.

One Sunday morning Mother came bursting into Sunday School saying, "Bill come quick, I can't find Bobby." The first thing we all thought of was that Bobby had somehow gotten into Panther Lake. We all spread out from the place where we were living and looked for him. He couldn't have gone far, he was just a toddler. When we found him he was happily on his way and had crossed the Benson Highway and was walking in the middle of the road pulling his little wagon to nowhere in particular. I don't think he even got a spanking. But he was sure smothered in kisses.

Another benefit of moving south of Renton was that I got my first taste of making money. I was around thirteen and during the summer, when we were out of school, my days were really boring. I slept late and my world was small, living in that place away from all my school friends and their activities. One morning while trying to sleep late I heard all this noise going on in the orchard just on the other side of our fence. It sounded like a big party with a tractor starting and stopping and kids yelling at the top of their voices. I dressed quickly and went out to investigate. Here were workers of all ages picking pie cherries and having a great time doing it.

I climbed over the fence and talked to some of the kids and they told me to go up to the barn and talk to a man regarding work. Mr. Roe had this crew of kids and young adults who worked for him. He contracted farmers in the East Hill area to pick their sour cherry crop for a fee. Then he hired a crew that was so large they could pick an orchard completely in a day or two.

Everyone was given a tall ladder with an extra leg that could be inserted into the middle of the tree, a shiny commercial pail with a hook on the handle to put the picked cherries in, and empty boxes were placed on the ground around the tree where you dumped the cherries you had picked. To learn to use your ladder was a bit of a trick and sometimes you had to have one of the experienced boys show you how to use it. Your ladder had two attached legs with the steps on it that were put at the outside of the tree and the single leg was put over the top of the tree and inserted in the soft dirt for stability almost like a tripod. You picked the section of the tree where you were standing and when that was finished you moved the two attached legs around the tree until you finished your tree and moved to the next one in line.

Mr. Roe paid his workers 1/4 of a cent per pound, which would be paid in cash on the last day of the picking season. We stripped the tree of every single cherry and boys riding a tractor with a sled behind it picked up our filled boxes and took them to the barn. After weighing our boxes of cherries, the weight was put on our tally.

This looked like a job I could handle, so I asked Mr. Roe if I could join his crew. He was glad I joined, as he always needed pickers. Some kids were not dependable and left on a whim. There was a constant turn over of pickers. He needed a large crew, actively picking to finish the job he had contracted to do. I went home and told mother about the job and assured her I would be fine and changed into my work clothes and started to work that day.

I got my friend Ruth Lievense to be my partner and we were a cherry-picking machine. We each had to pick 400 pounds of cherries a day to make one dollar. It took twenty large flats of cherries to make 400 pounds. Rising early Mother drove us or we walked to the next orchard if it wasn't too far and when we each earned a dollar we quit for the day. Seems like a lot of work to make only a dollar, but when you add up the dollars at the end of the season there was a lot of good old, cold cash.

Another benefit of working on this crew was that we met a lot of great boys. Mr. Roe hired only responsible kids. It would be easy for kids to get into throwing cherries at each other, causing havoc and not doing what he hired them for. For me, one boy working there was special. His name was Budd Smith but his first name was really Leonard. He went to Garfield High School in Seattle and played on their football team. After work, if the weather was nice, a bunch of us kids would get in cars and go to Lake Meridian to swim and goof around. Mother said I could go if I was with Budd and he brought me home before dinner. I developed a friendship with Budd that lasted several years.

My sister Margie joined the crew when she realized how much money I was making. She found out it was not easy work though. You see there was a lot of dust stirred up by the tractor's activity and the juice from the ripe cherries mixed with dust that ran down our arms made a terrible mess. It was too dirty a job for Margie and she had to keep going to the bathroom to wash up or fix her hair. Eventually, it got too much for her and she went home before her first day was finished.

The amount of money I made that first year was sizeable and enough to buy a lovely suede jacket that I wore with pride. Margie wanted to borrow my jacket, but this was one thing I had worked hard for and I refused to share with her or anyone else. I continued to work for Mr. Roe several years after that and we developed a great friendship.

I also picked strawberries and raspberries wherever I heard they needed pickers. I tried to pick peas down in the Kent valley, but I was fired for picking peas that were not mature enough to send to the cannery or even make a big king size stir-fry.

When I was fifteen and Ruth Lievense sixteen we went down to Kent to try to get work at Libby McNeil & Libby, a large commercial cannery that hired seasonal workers to can string beans. A small group was also hired to work with some specialty products. Ruth and I stood in a mob of workers and hoped they would pick us when management came out on a raised platform to announce the need of workers.

Both Ruth and I were lucky enough to be chosen together. In the employment office we had to fill out our applications, plus show our Social Security cards. Neither of us had a card so we were sent to the post office to get them. Workers qualified for a card only if they were sixteen and I being fifteen knew I was too young to apply. I put the date of my birth down on my application as Oct. 13, 1921 making me sixteen. Just a little lie surely wouldn't hurt much would it? Now days as soon as a baby is born he is issued a Social Security number and the government keeps track of him until he dies.

Back in the plant, Ruth and I were put in different areas. I worked on a conveyer belt with about six other women. The moving belt shook the beans so we could see to pick out the cut beans that still had stems on them or were cut too long. The last gal on the belt pushed the beans in the cans as they moved onto a circular apparatus and they were sealed and moved into the pressure cookers.

The rejected beans were mashed up and made into baby food. Ruth worked in another area where they canned raspberry specialties. We worked the entire string bean season and were happy with the money we made. When the season was over they let most of the people go, but no one said anything to me about not coming back. So I continued the next week to come back bright and early each day and worked the one belt still operating to can the straggler string beans.

At the end of the week when they gave out our pay checks, the office worker wanted to know how come I was still working when I should have stopped work a week before. I told her no one told me not to come, so I assumed they wanted me to finish my job. That was my last week at Libby McNeil & Libby.

By the way, the Social Security Office finally caught up with me 70 years later when my husband Glen died and I was in the process of filing papers to receive his Social Security. I received a card that the Social Security application dates I gave them did not agree with the records they had regarding my age. I had to go to the Social Security Office here in Silverdale and tell the truth, that I had lied. Be sure your sins will find you out.

Once I found out how many jobs were available, I began to look for jobs that I could handle. At Christmas time, J. C. Penney hired young people for the season's rush. I was hired and worked in the Renton Penney's store. I learned how to write out the sale on a ticket and then place the transaction with the money in a cup. I shot it like a slingshot on a wire to the business office in the balcony. The transaction was checked and any money to return to the customer was put in the little cup and sent back to my department.

We were not restricted to any area in the store, except the shoe department and were instructed to wander around looking for helpless and confused male customers. I remember that the men would buy just about anything for their wives, and by Christmas Eve the shelves were completely bare. I didn't work after Christmas so I don't know how many disappointed wives brought their sheets or towels back.

I also got a job in an ice creamery and I loved this job. I worked part-time on the weekends while I was in high school and some while in college during the summer. I was on call whenever someone didn't come to work or if it was warm and they were really busy. We could eat all we wanted of ice cream floats, cokes, and whatever they sold. It didn't take long though to get my fill of all those sweet things.

Chapter 5

Daddy taught Margie to play chords on the piano so she could accompany the singing at our prayer meetings. Margie had a real gift for playing the piano and could play any song, if you just hummed the tune she could follow you. Upstairs in bed at night when I was trying to sleep, I could hear Marge and Daddy playing down stairs in the front room into the wee hours of the morning. What fun they had and a real special musical bond was established between them.

When we purchased the appliances for our new home the folks went to a most unlikely place in Renton to purchase them.. We got our power from Puget Sound Power & Light Company and they sold hot water tanks, stoves and refrigerators too. You could purchase these things from them and pay for them monthly on your light bill. That was way before all the handy electric appliances we have now that are sold even in the drug store.

Our telephone was just off the kitchen at the top of the stairs leading to the basement. It was a long brown box with a ringer on the right side. You picked up the receiver and rang the ringer and the operator would say, "Number please?" We were on a party line and it was not unusual to break into and listen in on our neighbor's conversations.

Our house was heated by sawdust. We had a Risden Stoker in the basement with a large hopper that had to be kept full of sawdust. Uncle George was connected in some way with the man who invented this method of heating. It was a very inexpensive way to heat our house and had a nice even heat. The lumber industry in our area produced a lot of sawdust and being a waste product it was also a cheap way to heat. I guess you'd call it heating "green."

We had a full basement in the house with a shower, sink and toilet. In the winter it was always nice and warm down there and we boarded a man who in turn did Daddy's chores for him. I don't remember where he had his bed, or kept his belongings. He helped both Mother and Daddy with anything that needed to be done 24 hours a day.

One of his favorite chores was to care for our Jersey cow with her big beautiful eyes, and an easy going disposition. She was so gentle and easy to milk. Her stall was in the old house on the property and she didn't seem to mind that the floor was off kilter. On a rare occasion when he wasn't able, Dorothy Ridgley, my girl friend and I milked her and we laughed so hard we spilled all but a few drops of milk and came into the house with an empty bucket.

In our basement we had a cool-room for the milk just like everyone else did. We poured the milk into large bowls, and the cream settled on the top waiting to be skimmed before we used the milk for drinking. Mother used the thick cream for making whipping cream, and also to mix in the cottage cheese that she had made from the skim milk. Our Jersey cow's milk had a high butterfat rating so the milk was rich and delicious when it was cold.

We didn't have chickens in a pen but we did have Bantam chickens running around the place and we would find their nests and bring the eggs in to Mother. If we missed a nest, the hen would surprise us with a flock of little chicks. One day Daddy brought home a small goat from a friend and it seemed that all she did was eat weeds around the place. We had fun playing with her though and whenever Aubrey, the boy who lived with us, would lean over she would jump up on his back or buck him in the bottom. City kids missed out on so many different experiences that we took for normal.

Daddy had heard about the Pacific Gold peaches developed especially for our area and he put in several acres of them. It was a big undertaking for Daddy, who also had so much responsibility in the telephone company. He was the wire chief over Renton, Kent, Auburn, Enumclaw, Buckley, Black Diamond and what they called the East Lead up into the mountains and over to Eastern Washington. In the winter it wasn't unusual for him to get a call in the middle of the night and he had to get men out on a job or solve the problem himself. Snow in the mountains always meant Daddy would be gone for several days.

Occasionally, when my daddy was working in Kent I would go grocery shopping with him. I loved to help him because he not only got the items Mother told him to get, but picked up things that caught his eye. He had a sweet tooth just like I did and when we got home the grocery sacks had their share of goodies. He had a favorite Nabisco cookie and you could be sure he would have one or two packages in his grocery bags.

The young man who bagged our groceries knew Daddy. In fact everyone knew Daddy wherever he went. Daddy introduced me to Johnny Pike who came from a nice Christian family in the Kent area. He started to come to our house to visit on a regular basis and when my birthday came he brought me an unexpected present. It was a beautiful pair of white leather figure ice skates. What a surprise. I was afraid Mother wasn't going to let me keep them, but in this case she did. She was pretty sure I wouldn't be using them on a daily basis or going to ice rinks without telling her. What a wonderful gift. I know he worked a long time and saved his money to get them for me. I used those skates for many years on Panther Lake and have no idea who I gave them to when I got older. I hope they enjoyed those skates as much as I did.

Now something about the Pacific Gold peaches that Daddy grew. Of course I am loyal to the brand that we had in our orchard and to this day I've never tasted a peach that is as delicious. When I'd tell people that it was a semi-cling peach they were usually turned off. But the inconvenience of opening it differently is minor compared to the taste.

It's sweet with a bright peach color flesh and a peel that does not have to be blanched to remove. If you know how to get the pit out you have it made. You grasp the peach in your two hands after having run a knife around the peach, and turn your hands opposite ways. The two halves are instantly in different hands. A flick of your knife removes the pit. Then you take your knife and get a corner of the skin and it comes right off. There now, you know how to open them and if you can find some growing you should by all means try them.

Mother was the chief inspector and packer of our peaches. At harvest time, in the summer her headquarters was in our cool basement where the boxes with "W J Cross' Pacific Gold Peaches" labels on the ends were made by Daddy in his spare time. Only peaches without blemish were packed. Those that were not sold were put on the discard pile.

I've seen people stop after purchasing their peaches and pick over some on the discard pile to take home. Of course they were good to eat and made wonderful jams and preserves but my folks wouldn't sell anything marred or not top grade.

On weekends Daddy took Margie and me to a wide place on Empire Way along Lake Washington Boulevard. He set up a small stand and we were left to sell peaches. We always ran out of peaches, as they were so beautiful and they were priced more reasonably than the grocery store's peaches. I found one empty box in later years with the label that said "W J Cross Pacific Gold Peaches" and I had the label made into a picture and gave it to my brother Bob, as he was the only Cross descendant on our side and I wanted him to have it as a keepsake.

Mother also canned peaches, made jam and used them in desserts that were delicious. Whenever we had company we always had a dessert ready; canned peaches with whipped cream piled on top. Oh, I miss those peaches.

Mother kept county kids and we had one family in particular, the Sullivan's. The oldest girl was Grace, and then came Lucille. There were others in the family but they stayed with other people. When we got Lucille she was so neglected she would just lie in her bed all day. Mother worked with her and got her up, taught her to walk and talk and she began to behave normally. However, when she was old enough to go to school her teacher was not able to teach her and sent a note home to Mother saying she had tried but failed every effort.

Glen also tried to teach her the A, B, C,' s by using Scrabble tiles, but no matter how hard he tried, she was unable to know A from C. She was a loving child and we loved her and treated her like our little sister. One day without warning, the caseworker came and took her away from us.

They were going to put her in some school to see if she would respond to specialized training. It was a terrible shock for me to have her taken away so abruptly, what must it have been for her. In my mind I still remember her skipping from the house with her small suitcase and not looking back. I have cried many times remembering how cruel it was to do that to her. How could I have stopped that from happening?

Mother also kept two boys occasionally. One named Presley Roberts and the other Aubrey Cheek. They were both nice boys but their parents were just having a hard time and could not afford to keep them. Presley was given my bedroom and I wasn't very happy about that. Aubrey came at a different time and left our place and went to Grandma LaDukes place because there was more room and work to do there. During harvest time, he came over to our place to help in the orchard. Both boys milked our cow and helped with the chores whenever they were at our house. We appreciated them, as they were both nice boys and reliable workers.

After I was married and I lived with the folks during the war, while Glen was in Europe, I kept Marian a pretty little blond girl, whose mother needed a place for her to stay during summer vacation while she worked.

When I got her, she had the most terrible case of impetigo, a scabby skin disease all over her body, that the doctor had ever seen. I took her periodically to him and he used light treatments on her head and gave me a purple medication to apply all over her body. She did get better but it was a struggle. I took her to visit her mother at her work in Seattle one day and I felt so sorry for Marian. Her mother treated her so impersonal showing no signs of affection toward her at all. Some years later, I read Marian drowned while boating with some kids over in the Kirkland area of Lake Washington. Such a loss.

When we moved from Seattle to Uncle George's garage on Panther Lake we started to attend a small mission church located near the main train tracks in Renton. There were only a few members in the church and our family and the LaDukes with their daughter Patricia Jane were a welcome addition.

The pastor Brother Cady, was a single young man. When he spoke his bow tie bobbled up and down on his Adams apple and us kids thought it was so funny we could hardly contain ourselves. The first time we attended church, Grandma LaDuke spoke up and said "Hazel will sing for you." Mother was so embarrassed and protested that she was not a singer.

After that we started to attend another church on 3rd and Burnett, and it was also a storefront building on another railroad track. This church was an Assembly of God mission and our minister was Sister Finch, an older lady. She was a very good speaker who came from the Yakima area. Her three granddaughters spent summer vacations with her and Margie and I became real close friends with the Finch girls.

Northwest Bible College would send students each Sunday to help with the meetings in this little church and sometimes a student would preach. They were so afraid to stand up in front of that small group of people, probably for the first time, and would make so many mistakes. One time a young Bible student was telling about the woman who bowed at Jesus' feet and "washed his head with the hair of her feet." She never knew what she'd said but we got a big kick out of it. We'd get the giggles so bad it was hard to stop. Can you imagine getting a laugh at the same joke for over 70 years?

One young student named Orland could not control his knee when he spoke and it would shake back and forth the whole time he was talking. We didn't laugh at him though, as he was trying so hard. His sister Priscilla, was also a student who eventually married another student Bill McNutt and they became our pastors in the little church our men built in Renton on the south side of Cedar River.

My dad bought an old White Milk Delivery Truck and besides using it on our place he used it to take our family down to camp meeting at Borst Park in Centralia during the summer. When we'd drive down the park's road where people had pitched their tents, Daddy would honk the horn and we'd yell and wave to everyone that we were back. How happy we were to be there at camp meeting, seeing kids we met the year before. They came from all over the state of Washington and even from up in British Columbia.

There was a large temporary wooden tabernacle in the middle of the camp where the evening meetings were held and the floor had either plain dirt or sawdust. What good times we had at those meetings. The singing was glorious and testimonies wonderful. Those were the days when we would see demonstrations of God's mighty power. The voices of hundreds of people in that tabernacle raised a great volume of praise and you could just feel the power of God permeating the praise of His people.

At night after the service a large group of young people would gather around the piano to sing and fellowship with one another. Notable speakers were featured, such as Charles S. Price, who had been a preacher in a large main-line church and left his church after being filled with the Spirit of God and called to be an evangelist. Those were the days of tent revivals too.

A group of churches in a city would sponsor a city wide evangelistic effort for a week or so. It was not unusual to have these meetings continue another week because there was such a response to the messages. I remember one speaker who was an artist who drew a chalk picture while giving his message and then he gave the picture away to someone. His pictures were always really beautiful and his pictures would draw many, in hopes they would receive one of the pictures. He and his wife stayed with Grandma and Grandpa LaDuke on the chicken ranch, during their crusade.

It was at one of these camp meetings that I met a couple of boys at the horseshoe pit and played several games with them. After the meeting that night as kids were singing around the piano, Margie met one of the boys I had played horseshoes with that day. It was Phil Youngquist who she married several years later. I didn't mind as she was more his type than I was.

Grandpa LaDuke went with us to a revival in Tacoma in a large temporary structure. They had sawdust on the floor and Grandpa LaDuke felt more at ease there than a regular church, as he could spit his tobacco juice on the floor and cover it up with the sawdust. Grandpa LaDuke had chewed tobacco for many years and we accepted it as just what he did. I hardly ever saw him without a chaw in the side of his cheek.

Right after these meetings he sent me to Eddings Gas Station about a block from his ranch to get him some tobacco. When he got the plug he took a big bite and immediately spit it out. It tasted terrible to him. In one bite the Lord had delivered him from that nasty stuff. He never chewed tobacco again. That was a real miracle.

About that time Stella Moore started a 4-H sewing club. A few of us girls who wanted to learn to sew joined her club. We met in a lady's home next door to Stella's because it was much larger than the Moore's house and able to accommodate a group of girls working on several different projects. Our motto was "Head, Hand, Heart and Health," and what it meant I'm sure I didn't know.

We had " Beginning Sewing" my first year. Stella showed us the basics and we advanced each year to more difficult projects. From a plain little dishtowel to a blue wool dress, I advanced through the courses. If we received a ribbon of any kind at a local fair then we could go to the state fair and compete in the 4-H exhibit there. My last year, I won first place in sewing and modeling my blue wool dress at the state 4-H contest at the Yakima County Fair.

Chapter 6

I went to Renton Jr. High the year we moved into Uncle George's place and to get the five miles to school we rode on an old stage (bus) owned by Bill Thompson Sr. Bill was married to Lydia and was father to Lois and Billy. When Lydia had her first baby it was stillborn and a young woman in the hospital at the same time was not able to care for her little girl so the Thompson's adopted her baby and they came home from the hospital with baby Lois. For years folks didn't know that Lois wasn't their biological child. Lois was a beautiful little girl who had such a happy disposition. When she grew up, matured and married she was a sweet Christian wife and mother. Both Bill and Lydia had done a fine job in raising Lois, a little baby who was not wanted.

Lydia played the piano for church services while she was carrying their boy Billy and we all watched expectantly for him to be born. As I was saying, Bill Thompson Sr. drove us to school in that old stage. It had plush seats, a low ceiling and an extra big fat tire on the back of the bus. The kids didn't fool with Bill or cause trouble on his bus. If they did, Bill kicked them off and told them to walk home.

One afternoon on the way home from school, he got fed up with a kid's actions, stopped the bus and took him by the shoulders, true to his word, and put him off. That was a good lesson for all the loud mouth kids who rode Bill's stage.

Those of us who could see the big old tire knew that when Bill started up the stage the kid grabbed on to the tire on the back and rode it home like a bronco. Some thought Bill never knew the kid was holding on, but with the look on Bill's face most of us knew his secret. No one fooled Bill, at least on his stage.

I loved Junior High School. I thought I was so big. The school was next door to the new Renton High and both of them together were beautiful schools with large play fields and tracks behind them. I loved sports and turned out for whatever they offered for girls. Most of the sport opportunities however were for boys only. I did enter into races on the track and loved the low hurdles because I had long legs and it was a piece of cake to vault them. I remember one of the races when I blacked out and a boy carried me into the school locker room. I had been running hard and the weather was rather warm. I have wondered since if it was a condition I now have called Tachy-Brady Syndrome, which is fast, and then slow heart beat.

I studied hard and got good grades in all my school years. On my free periods I worked in the office and thought I was meant more and more for the business world. The office manager had confidence in me and allowed me to type the tests for the teachers. I remember with shame, giving Margie the answers to one of her tests. To this day I recall how I failed the office manager's confidence.

I tried out for a play and was not picked for an acting part, but they did need someone to crow like a rooster and of course I could do that because as you remember I was a chicken farmer's granddaughter.

When I got to high school I became active in everything I could qualify for. At the last minute a girl who was in a one-act play the school was putting on got sick and the drama teacher asked me to learn the girl's part in just a few short days. I memorized it quickly and the play proceeded as if the girl had been there.

Another production we put on in the school, there was a scene where a group of people would come out on the stage and dance as though they were at a ball. Well my girlfriend, Margie Axelson, let me wear her red satin full-length dress and I thought it looked so good on me that I was thrilled to be included. When it came time for our group to dance the boy I was to dance with could not be found, so I just went out and danced by myself. Now I had on that beautiful dress and felt I just had to perform in it. You would have done the same too, wouldn't you? For some reason the drama teacher was not pleased.

My friend Margie Axelson lived on the Benson Highway several miles from our house. Their house was on a corner and it had a tall chain link fence surrounding their property, as they had two Great Dane dogs that ran freely in the yard. Whenever I visited her, I had to wait at the gate for her to come out to the gate and escort me in. I was so afraid of those dogs as they were almost as big as I was. One day when I was over at her house we wanted something sweet to eat, so we decided to make some candy. It turned out a mess and she was afraid to leave it where her mother might find it, so we took it out in the back yard and dug a hole and buried it. We never did know if the dogs dug it up or if her mother found out.

When I was a junior in High School I tried out for cheerleader. I practiced and practiced and when the time came to do my stuff I had to run out onto the stage and lead everyone in a cheer. I choose the cheer "Rouse 'em, Renton, Souze 'em, Renton, Rouse 'em, Souze 'em Renton." And would you believe it, I made the cheer squad with a cheer like that? Then again in my senior year, I became the cheer queen. It was a real honor to be chosen on the cheer squad as we were privileged to go to all the events where we led cheers for our school's teams. Renton High School was good at sports and we had many winning years. My dad was so proud of me even if I didn't turn out to be a boy.

I was also on the Honor Society all through Junior High and High School and enjoyed going to various Honor Society events. It was unusual for me to try to impress anyone with my looks, but these occasions were special events and I wanted to look my best.

In my senior year I asked my sister Margie to fix my hair for the Honor Society breakfast. I had a hat that I got from someone and I wanted a hairstyle that would look good under the hat. Margie put my hair up in pin curls and when she combed it out the morning of the breakfast it went just every which way. We tried to tame it but to no avail. She did the best she could, but I was just ugly with her. I told her I thought she made a mess of my hair because she couldn't go to the breakfast. Good thing I had that hat to cover my hair. I'm sorry for how I treated my sister. The breakfast was held in the basement of the Episcopal Church and as usual we had a great time. The kids all wanted me to lead them in a cheer so I got up on the tabletop with my hat on and we all cheered for Renton High. So much for being a lady.

With graduation coming the student council met to prepare for what part the graduates would take in the ceremonies. They determined that we would have a boy and girl to speak on the subject of Washington State's 50th celebration of statehood. Our state was ratified in 1889, so in 1939 the state was 50 years old. The class was to vote on their choice of a boy and girl speaker by the criteria our class advisor gave.

Several students qualified, and Dick Hazel and I were chosen. The subject was "50 Years of Achievement." We met weekly with our advisor, in her home and worked on our speeches. How many weeks it took to write those speeches I do not remember but it was an arduous task. After we finished our speeches, memorizing them was not difficult as having worked on them so long, the words were imprinted in our minds.

The night of the graduation we were all terribly excited. The girls wore long white gowns and the boys wore dark suits, white shirts and black ties. Most of the girls had a lovely corsage and some of the boys a boutonniere. I received two lavender orchids from my friend Budd Smith. He also gave me a gold heart necklace that had a diamond in it. It was beautiful and I was so pleased. It just set off my long white chiffon dress with ruffles around the low neck.

I was so excited and I remember the feeling of exhilaration in being part of the program. My speech was delivered perfectly and I didn't use the prompter once. Afterwards in the gym, Dorothy Ridgley and I hugged each other and cried. She was my very best friend. It was Dorothy who got me interested in fixing my hair and trying to be more lady-like. She was a pretty girl with beautiful hair. When she graduated from school she went to Beauty College to get her license as a beautician. She had a natural knack at fixing hair and taught me how to put pin curls in. She had fixed my hair for graduation and it was just the way I liked it. We knew we were going different ways and were so afraid we would drift apart.

That is just what happened. I went to college and she got a job in a beauty salon in Renton. One time I did meet her when I was waiting for the bus in front of the Bon Marche and showed her my engagement ring. I did see her several times at class reunions, but then it was many years before I was able to find her again in Sequim, in an assisted living home. We were both in our 70's.

Now about Budd Smith, my friend I'd known since cherry-picking days. He was one of the boys on the tractor and we both were sweet on each other at first sight. You know how that is. There is always that special attraction that draws people together. I was several years younger than he and I think he was ahead of me in school. He was a lineman on the varsity football team for Garfield High and knew many of the players who went on to play for the University of Washington.

One night one of these guys, Johnny Boitano and Budd came to pick me up on a date. You know a date that is double with only one girl. Budd had no transportation and he had to take whatever was the best arrangement. Johnny had this old car that they had just fixed up, so that's why Budd came with Johnny. After our night together, probably a football game or some other athletic event, on coming home up the Benson Hill road the car stalled. On close examination, the guys discovered they had put the distributor in backwards and the gas was pumped away from the engine rather than to it. They both horsed around and fixed it and they finally got me home.

Budd went to church with me at the 3rd & Burnett mission and gave his heart to the Lord. His family was really different from mine. He had an older father who did not work and stayed home and worked around the house. His mother was the breadwinner and had a regular boyfriend. One night, when I was at Budd's house with him, his mother introduced me to her friend. They were going out, and Budd's dad would be staying home to wash clothes. I didn't like the looks of that situation.

I wasn't a mushy girl and I got tired of Budd kissing me all the time. However, I did enjoy the gifts he brought me such as boxed chocolates. Ymm. I have always felt bad for the way I treated Budd. He was not to blame for his family and he was a clean handsome guy.

I especially liked his curly, black, shiny hair and the freckles on his face. He had a good build and wasn't a wimp. After I graduated from high school, one night after church we walked down the railroad tracks to talk. I had been giving him the cold shoulder and I knew he was hurt. He asked me if I would rather he not come to see me any more and I said, "Yes." That was one of the last times I had a talk with him. When he was older he got a job in the telephone company and married a nice Christian girl and lived in the Port Townsend or Port Angeles area.

Now, in defense of my actions toward Budd, I was going to start Seattle Pacific College and expected a complete change in my life and I wanted to be free to date other boys. Also, I had had a great family who loved each other and when I got serious about a guy, I wanted his family to be a good example like my family I hoped would be to our children when we had them. I have dreamt about Budd many times in my life since then and on waking felt bad for my actions. I should have handled it in a kinder way. I hoped to see him again so I could apologize but did not. I have prayed for the Lord's forgiveness and I believe He has forgiven me for my unchristian like actions.

Chapter 7

Now how in the world did I decide to go to Seattle Pacific College? Washington State College was my first choice as I had been there for a week's convention for 4-H and liked what I saw. I wanted to major in Business Administration even though I knew WSC wasn't strong in this field. I sent my application to their admittance office and received a rejection because somehow I failed to fulfill the requirement for a science in high school. So I went out to the University of Washington with the hopes that maybe they would take me. The outcome was the same. I was really frustrated. I had had very good grades through high school and I couldn't even find a college that would accept me.

My folks had invited a couple that attended our church one Sunday to come home for dinner and during the conversation my mother mentioned my quandary. The young lady told mother she had graduated from Seattle Pacific College and if I tried, possibly I would be accepted. We had never heard of the school but the first opportunity we had, Mother took me to SPC. It was so small compared to the U of W or WSC but I liked the beautiful campus and the friendly way they considered my situation.

The Bursar, Harry Ansted, was also the Professor of Economics and Business and upon showing him my application and telling him my rejection stories, he said it would be possible for me to attend if I made up my science by taking a mathematics class without credit. And that is just what I did. I was finally duly enrolled in college at the ripe old age of sixteen.

My first roommate was Doris Dykeman, a girl from Puyallup Valley. Her family owned a Bible book store there. We both admitted we were scared to see what the other would be like. We got along great. She had her doubts though when she first saw me come into our room with a hat on. Was I trying to hide my hair or just be fashionable?

In our room, beside the regular furniture provided by the school, we had a small three legged table with a skirt around it where we kept my coffee pot and the fixings for coffee and other treats. The rules of Tiffany Hall were that we could do no cooking in our rooms. Who can study late at night without something to eat or drink? There was a small bakery facing our campus and students were frequent customers.

One night while we were studying, I got to thinking of those great raised doughnuts sold in that bakery. The door to Tiffany Hall was locked early in the evening and our Preceptress Miss Lillian Pickens' apartment was just inside the main door. No one came in or out without Miss Pickens seeing them. So to get out and over to the bakery I would have to find another way.

At the end of our hall in the dorm, a window opened to the fire escape and that was the way I chose. So I started the coffee to brew and hurrying to the bakery, I purchased all the girls' pastry requests and climbed back up the fire escape to the window entry.

I heard Miss Pickens coming, so I ducked inside the girl's closet in the room closest to the fire escape and stuck my head out and said, "She didn't catch me did she." Who do you suppose was standing in the doorway of the room but our sly Miss Pickens. Her only words to me were "I'll see you in my office tomorrow morning Miss Cross." I should have known she'd smell the coffee. The next day wasn't nearly as bad as my worries all night had been.

I took geometry as my make-up mathematics from Dr. Burton Beegle and passed with an average grade. I didn't put too much effort into the course, as my Business Administration classes required so much reading. Dr. Beegle was a likeable geometry teacher and he kept his students awake in class by whacking his pointer stick on the blackboard at a quiet time. We never failed to jump to attention.

Also I helped pay for my tuition by working in the Bursar's office at various times in the day. My French teacher, Dr. Golda Kendrick, literally loved her subject and I enjoyed the class best when she taught us French songs. I took French for two years and my French is limited to a few mispronounced words. Another teacher I enjoyed was Miss Lillian Danielson who taught speech. She spoke so loud and clear we could hear her in the office above her classroom saying "Ship Ahoy." Miss Mabel Shipley the History professor, who I never had the privilege of having for a teacher, took me aside one day and asked me to please not be so loud and un-lady like when I led cheers.

They had never had official cheerleaders or majorettes at SPC before and in my sophomore year Jean Sarvas, LaVerne Engebretsen and myself were asked by Professor Hardwick Harshman to be joint cheer and majorette leaders for the band. We had to get our own uniforms, which we made from a shiny red and white satin material with the skirt hemline below our knees. We found batons some place and were in business. We pranced around the basketball court and I probably would die laughing now at how funny we must have looked.

I also worked in the kitchen of Tiffany Hall after dinner, the location of the school's dining room. We all ate family style at large tables seating ten students and when the serving plates were returned to the kitchen I put food leftovers in gallon cans for possible use later. Servers started the food to the left on the tables and if your seat was the last one on the right, possibly some guy would empty the entire contents on his plate and then pass the empty serving dish to you. You would have to wait until the server stood in line and got a refill before you got your portion. This was a mean trick guys loved to play on the girls.

Eating family style dinner had to be at an exact time and everyone would stand at his or her place until after grace was said. If you came late while someone was praying, you waited outside the entrance until the prayer was finished and everyone sat down.

There was one guy who was always late, and you could be sure he would be waiting at the glass door after grace was said. His name was Glen Odle, the brother of my friend Ardis Odle who lived near me in the dorm. Glen had a job in the dining room too and used a small brush to sweep the crumbs into a small pan after the dishes were removed from the table. I got to know him a little and I was very unimpressed. I would also see him running around with a stack of books under his arm, probably late for some class. He was a good tennis player though, and I would see him too, when I watched the tennis team practice.

We had a wonderful time at SPC. They had so many activities geared for the different classes and all school events. Dinners, skating parties, sports events, boat trips and other fun things. Because we were a small school everyone was invited to most of the events and we got to know most of the students who lived in the dorms. One of the boys, Jim Isaac, who sat at my dinner table, went to an Assembly of God Church, and because we had our church in common we'd talk more freely. I knew that the Freshman Salmon Bake in Edmonds was coming on February 2nd and assumed Jim would ask me.

Was I surprised when he asked if I'd like to go with Glen Odle. I hardly even knew Glen and besides, I saw him talking to Charlotte Anderson and thought he'd take her. I didn't know Jim had been talking to Glen about me and had been trying to match us up. Disappointed, I said yes I'd go with Glen, but I really wanted to go with Jim. So the date was arranged and the day of the beach party was as nice as a day in February could be. We went to Edmonds and the area of the bake is totally commercialized today. No buildings or businesses were along the beach in Edmonds in those days.

We had a lovely sandy spot where the cooks had buried the salmon on hot coals beneath the sand. We sat on the sand to eat and what a great salmon dinner it was. It didn't take all of us long to get acquainted as we sat around the fire on the beach and sang songs.

The date of the all school skate conflicted with the opening date of the Seattle Rainier's baseball team. I was all excited about going skating, as I loved to skate. When I was in high school, Daddy used to take me and a few of my friends skating at Redondo Skating Rink. I had also skated on a cement tennis court when I was in grade school. Those were the days when you screwed your skates on the bottom of your shoes.

Well, Glen had promised to take me to the party although he really wanted to go to the ballgame. When it was time to leave for the party a fellow named Clayton Engebretsen came to pick me up. Surprised, and mad that Glen wasn't there, I went with Clayton and we had a great time but Glen was sure in the doghouse.

These were serious and unsettling days for young people. Many were leaving school to join up with the troops. Hitler was setting out to make the amazing race by eliminating the Jews. War was on the horizon. Special church services for college students were held in the Free Methodist Church across the street from SPC. We had a speaker who was encouraging those who were not sure of their commitment to Christ, to make sure, by coming forward to the altar. I was sitting on the main floor area and I had no idea where Glen was. Many of the students were coming forward from all over the sanctuary. I heard someone coming down the balcony stairs and down the main isle to the front of the audience. It was Glen and I was so glad as I didn't know how he stood spiritually.

Chapter 8

This was our sophomore year of school and Glen and I had gone steadily for nearly two years. I had visited his home in Bellevue and I was impressed with their family. His father, Mosie Frank Odle was born in West Frankfort, Illinois on December 11, 1888 to a hardworking family of farmers and coal miners. This area of Illinois is one that leads in the production of hard coal found deep in the earth. He was from a relatively large family and fortunate to be able to finish eighth grade. He took and passed a test that qualified him to teach school at that time.

Frank as he was called, was invited to come work with a cousin, who farmed wheat in the Horse Heaven area around Prosser and Grandview, Washington. He left his teaching job in Illinois to seek his fortune out West. He worked on a wheat farm for a while before going to Bellingham, seeking a teaching certificate. There he entered and graduated from Bellingham Normal School, one of Washington State's leading schools for teachers.

Mr. Odle began his teaching career in 1913, after graduating from Bellingham Normal School, teaching in a two-room schoolhouse in Getchell, a small rural community near Marysville, in Snohomish County. He met and married Inez Beulah Gibson, a fellow teacher. She too, passed a test to qualify for teaching before going on to Bellingham Normal. She was from a large Scandinavian family in the area, having three brothers and four sisters.

Frank then went to teach in Foster, in the outskirts of Seattle for several years until he was hired at Bellevue, a little town on the east side of Lake Washington. In 1918, Bellevue consisted of one street called Main, a small business district and the school where he was employed. Japanese truck farmers, who raised mostly peas and strawberries, farmed the area around the town. That area is now paved over and skyscrapers and shopping centers replace the farms that were once there. Bellevue was one of the areas that during World War II, the Japanese and their families were removed from their homes to internment camps because they were considered a threat to the security of the United States.

Frank and Inez bought a large two story family home with full basement on five acres of land in a grove of fir trees on 108th Avenue NE. That house where they raised their family is now just a few blocks from the middle of Bellevue. There was a large water tower behind their home that supplied the water for the complex, and a barn with a stall for the family cow that supplied their milk, cream and butter. Chickens were raised both for the eggs and consumption, while a pig was always kept to take care of kitchen scraps and to provide pork.

Although he was a hard-working schoolteacher, the farmer in him led him to raise a large garden, which produced vegetables for eating and canning for the winter months. The children helped to harvest the walnuts, quince, apples, pears and cherries from their orchard of nut and fruit trees. That home is still there today, preserved as a historical landmark.

The Odle family grew to five children. Philip Douglas their first, born in 1915, with the same calling as his parents, taught only one year in Warden, WA and one year in Poulsbo, WA before following his heart and becoming a musician.

Willard Franklin, the second son, born in 1917 excelled in school and after taking a course in chemistry and obtaining a master's degree, his heart's desire was to be a surgeon. Willard was drafted and scored the highest of those in his battalion, and he was given the option to be discharged and be sent to school for a degree in medicine or to remain in the service and be sent where they felt best. Willard applied at 30 dental schools and he was accepted first at the Pacific Dental School at the University of Oregon. He was discharged from the Army and he and his wife Eleanor moved to Portland where he attended dental school, graduating in three years, and then Willard had a long and successful practice in dentistry in Seattle where he and Eleanor raised their three children. The Odle's third son Glen was born in 1920 and suffered the pain of enduring long curls that his mother put in, as he was to have been their little girl.

Ardis Marian, the first girl in the Odle family was born in 1921 and attended Bellevue schools following her brothers to Seattle Pacific College with the hope of being a grade school teacher like her mother. She taught for one year at Elk Plain and one year in Medina, WA. She met Dick Ashton her freshman year at SPC and they were married in November, 1942. Dick was with the Lake Washington School District in the central office in Kirkland, and in his spare time he enjoyed designing and redecorating homes. Ardis was able to move into many lovely homes that Dick either remodeled or built.

Muriel, the last child of Frank and Inez was born in 1923 and attended SPC where she met Marshall Adams and married him in 1946 after he was separated from the Marines.

At his retirement in 1968, school directors honored Mr. Odle by giving his name to a new junior high that was under construction, Odle Junior High School, located at 14400 N.E. 4th Street in Bellevue. Governor Dan Evans who presented him the State's Distinguished Citizen Award also honored him. After his death, February 28, 1969, the Washington State House of Representatives honored Mr. Odle by passing HRC 14, paying tribute to him "as the man who had the longest teaching career (55 years) of anyone in the history of the state. Mr. Odle was the personification of excellence in education."

At the opening ceremonies of the Odle Junior High School, Senator Henry M. Jackson presented an American flag that had flown over the capitol building in Washington, D.C. and a large colored portrait of Mr. Odle saying "In paying tribute to Mr. Odle, we not only salute the person, we salute all the qualities he stood for as a true professional in the field of education – integrity, imagination, inspiration, a brilliant mind, physical fitness and overwhelming confidence in the ability of the individual to accomplish any task. Certainly, his almost 'log cabin' beginning is a tribute to these qualities."

In a telegram read at his memorial service, President Richard M. Nixon wrote: "M. Frank Odle's death is a loss not only to his family, but also to education in America and to the nation as a whole."

His interest in personal fitness was evidenced as he walked to and from school each day, a three-and-a-half mile round trip, and would walk a two mile round trip to get a haircut. He chopped the wood used to supplement his home's heat and in a newspaper article about Mr. Odle when he was 78 years of age, he was shown helping a family friend clearing some property of a stand of alder. Mr. Odle was planning to finish the project by the time school opened in the fall with what he figured to be a three-year supply of firewood. He scorned the use of power saws, preferring instead to use a big old-fashioned crosscut saw and an axe. He would say, "I don't want to just lie around, and kill time. I am the kind of person who feels better if I have something worth while to do." This was the kind of family I wanted to be part of.

Chapter 9

My sophomore year at SPC I roomed with two girls in a small apartment across from the campus on Nickerson Street. Margie Carlson, Laura Belle Smith and myself were great friends. Because I was having a tough time with chemistry one or the other would drill me on each day's material as we sat on the side of the bathtub early in the morning. We studied there so we'd not disturb those still sleeping.

I got an A in chemistry that year only because of all the help I received from the girls and because I turned in extra problems solved by going to after school help classes. The three of us managed to spend the entire year together in that little upstairs apartment. To get to our place you had to go through the owner's front room and up the stairs that ran along the wall to our apartment. No one could reach our apartment undetected.

There were times when we had boys over and if the homeowners were not home we would entertain the boys in their front room. I remember one time when the guys got a little rowdy while tossing a ball around the room and broke a lamp. We were horrified at what the owners might do and tried to repair the lamp. We got it together again but I don't think it was ever the same.

While we lived there, some guys who lived in an apartment in a house next door to us said they'd pay us if we'd wash their shirts and iron them. Always needing money, we jumped at the chance. We had no idea how many shirts they had, maybe five apiece, so we took on the job. When we got to their apartment, we found there was so many shirts we had to wash them in their bathtub. Thinking back, I wonder if those fellows were trying to make money off us by running a Chinese laundry?

After washing them, we dried them at our place and ironed them taking turns until we finally got the job finished. I wonder how much they paid us? Probably not much, knowing the financial condition of most college kids.

We'd go to Pike Place Market in downtown Seattle and get our produce. I think we spent approximately $10.00 each week for all the things we got there. Then I went home to our place in Renton on the weekend and Mother would send me back with a large shopping bag filled with fresh bread and many other good things to eat. I'm sure we also had some jars of peach jam and canned peaches. Pacific Gold, of course.

One evening, Glen and I had a very serious conversation. Because he was 21 he knew he would be drafted and wanted to know if I would wait for him. That seemed to be the question most guys asked their girlfriends. Arriving home, I couldn't shake his question to me, so I found a place and knelt and prayed to the Lord whether or not I should commit myself to him. Shocked that the answer was a negative, I rejected God's leading. Glen and I were such good friends and seemed to be on the same wavelength. Also, I was so impressed by his family. It was just the kind of Christian family I wanted to be part of. I don't remember ever giving him an answer to his question and we continued being close friends. Looking back, what I should have done was continue in school and follow God's leading. But as usual, I was stubborn and wanted my own way.

Glen had been working at the gas station at 3rd and Nickerson during school and as soon as school was out our sophomore year he got a job working for Pacific Northwest Bell. He thought he should establish himself in a good company before entering the service. I also got a job working for PNB in the directory department, proofreading the telephone book. Talk about a boring job, but at least I had a job. I didn't last long there as an opportunity opened up in the order department, typing phone service contracts for new accounts. Typing was always my forte and I was happy there until I heard the Boeing Airplane Company was looking for clerk typists. I got a job in the McDermott Building in the Engineering Department typing cover letters for blueprints that were being sent to Wichita, Kansas. They had an underground vault there, to put the plans for a new Navy airplane the XPBB1 that Boeing was experimenting on. I got twice as much pay working for Boeing as the phone company.

My boss was a Christian man named Irving Carlson and he put a new hire in the next desk from me. Our typewriters faced each other and of course we had to get acquainted. Her name was Doris Johnson and she had come from Bismarck, North Dakota with her sister and a couple of other girls. She turned out to be a Christian also and we became close friends. Our boss Irving was not happy with all our talking but we both produced as much or more work than the other girls. My friendship with Doris lasted for more than 50 years and our precious relationship was only separated by her death.

One day at work an announcement was delivered over the loudspeaker system to stop all work in Engineering on the XPBB1 flying boat as it was determined it had to fly too low to engage the enemy, putting our vessels and submarines in jeopardy. What a shock to all the employees as we had guarded our blueprints so carefully and now all the blueprints were taken out of our vaults and put in large trash cans to be disposed of.

It took only a short time before our Engineering Department was back to work on a new plane, the B-29 that they had secretly been working on. This plane proved to be an advanced model of the B-17 with greater capacity in every area. I was still working for Boeing when World War II began, and our lives took on a whole new direction.

Chapter 10

Our fall had been really chilly and now the temperatures were in the freezing range. Just a few more days and Panther Lake would be frozen enough for us to skate on. Panther Lake, about five miles south of Renton was a small shallow lake and it didn't take much for it to freeze. When we were kids, Daddy would take a long pole with him as he skated over the lake to test conditions before he'd let us skate on it. We enjoyed this pretty little lake more in the winter than summer, as the lake's bottom was filled with silt and mushy stuff with cattails growing along the shore. It was impossible to wade along the shore in the summer, as each step you took, your feet would sink down, down, down. But in winter when it froze, we could venture out immediately.

There were also several areas northeast of our home that had uncultivated fields with standing water in the winter, and when the fields froze they were almost as good to skate on as the lake. Being just surface ice it was less dangerous too. Everyone called it the "Japs" place because they owned those fields and as far as seeing the owners, we never did. These areas were always teaming with people when the fields froze and young families brought their little kids to this area to teach them to skate. The bigger kids used the larger cleared off areas to play ice hockey.

I learned to skate on Panther Lake with the help of a boy named Dennis who was determined I'd get my ankles upright instead of turned in towards each other. He'd take me firmly in hand and before I knew it we were smoothly skating over the ice. Fires were built on the shore and a few old logs were placed where we could sit, put on our skates and then take off over the ice.

In the winter of 1941 we had a hard freeze and one night, Glen brought his younger sister Middy with him to skate. Eric Carlson, an older friend of ours was there, and took Middy with him to skate around the lake. They got into some thin ice on the far side and fell through. Fortunately, they were able to get out of the water by themselves but they were both soaking wet and shivering in the cold. Our home was probably two or three blocks away and we got them there and warmed up as quickly as we could. Mother gave them something hot to drink and rustled up some dry clothes for them to wear.

Skating at night, when you can't see exactly where you're going, is really dangerous. I remember skating alone on the ice more than once, going as fast as I could to get back to shore because the ice was cracking under my skates. All it would have taken was for me to stumble on a twig and I would have been long gone. I am so fortunate that I escaped having a terrible accident because I was so foolish to take such chances.

The road along the front of our ten acres had a gradual slope and when it snowed it was great to get several kids on your sled and go whipping down the hill. Now no one drove this hill when it snowed, as it was just too steep to make it up or down without chains. Trudging up this hill on foot before sliding down was a real workout. We'd come home with rosy cheeks and red noses. Wow, we'd have great fun.

Glen visited me in the afternoon of December 7, 1941 to take me skating and when I met him at the door he asked if I'd heard the news that the Japanese had bombed Pearl Harbor. I had heard the news and all the speculation that now we would be at war with Japan and not in Europe. President Roosevelt called it "a date that will live on in infamy," and he declared war on Japan on Dec. 8, 1941. The Japanese had sunk or damaged nineteen ships and 2,300 of our men were killed. Germany and Italy declared war on the U.S. and on December 11, 1941 we responded with a declaration of war against them later the same day. This was developing into the "big one" and soon the whole world would be engaged in some way in the Second World War.

Within a short time Congress introduced the draft and single men were conscripted into the military service. Glen was working for the telephone company when he got his call for that first draft after Pearl Harbor. He tried desperately to get in the Navy with the help of some Navy friends but in February 1942 he had to report to the Army at Fort Lewis. I went with his folks when he was inducted and saw first hand how war affects not only the participants but also the whole family. It was the beginning for all of us of over four long years of uncertainty and distress. It was a time when we would be separated without knowing if we'd ever be together again.

Before Glen left for the Army we had gone shopping in Seattle to pick out my engagement ring. We were caught up in the hysteria of the time while trying to live normally in the face of the excitement of war and not knowing the future. In Ben Tipp's jewelry store across from the Bon Marche on 2nd and Pike we found a lovely diamond. I was thrilled. We decided I wouldn't wear my ring until some romantic moment when Glen would put it on my finger. I had to go to the bathroom after leaving Ben Tipp's so we stopped at Woolworth's ten-cent store, a block from Ben Tipp's. While I was in the stall, I took the ring out of my purse to look at it again and couldn't resist putting it on my finger. On joining Glen later, I showed him I had the ring on my finger. That must have been our romantic moment. He didn't care if I had the ring on now or later just so I pledged my life to him. When we got to the folks' place we happily showed mother my ring and she was so disappointed. Her reaction was like putting a pin in a balloon.

She hadn't wanted me to be engaged until I finished college. I was only nineteen, with two years to go in school and everything was happening too fast for her. Somehow, I didn't connect having a ring with the first step in getting married. I was in a whirl of excitement like so many young girls and was thrilled to have a beautiful engagement ring to show off. Mother on the other hand had eloped with daddy and had missed the fun of bridal showers and the memories of a beautifully planned wedding. She didn't want me to have the same disappointment.

Before we knew it, Glen was off to war on a troop train and he wouldn't have much time to spend writing letters to me. I pledged to write him though every day, to keep him informed with news from home. All over the country the war effort was gearing up and our country was changing from producing cars and trucks to guns and ammunition and anything needed for the military in time of war.

The government started to ration groceries, meat, shoes, gas, tires and just about everything the military would need. I remember we obtained our coupon books from the ration board and when we purchased an item we had to spend not just our money but give a coupon as well.

It wasn't long before manufacturing cars and civilian trucks stopped all together. If you didn't have a vehicle then you'd have to wait until after the war to make your purchase or buy a used one. In busy public areas, a special area was roped off to hold stainless steel or aluminum pots and pans to recycle for building war items and almost everyone responded enthusiastically. We also bought war bonds, which was really lending the government our money at a low interest rate, redeemable after the war. It was not unusual to give a war bond for a gift.

Our shoes were resoled by the cobbler rather than buying new. Everywhere you went were signs "Uncle Sam Wants You." Women took the places of the men who had been drafted and "Rosie the riveter" wasn't just a song but she actually worked with a bandana around her head and dressed with overalls, taking the place of a man. Even my mother got a job at Boeing, working in the shop where tools were checked out. In all my life I can't remember my mother working outside the home before this effort began, especially with a pair of men's overalls on and a bandana on her head. The entire country was behind the war effort and songs and programs encouraged everyone to support our military forces. It was the ordinary people in our country who along with our military, helped to win the war with their unfailing love for our great country and with loyalty and willingness to respond without grumbling over our country's war effort.

In 1942, the Federal government began forcibly moving 110,000 Japanese-Americans from the West Coast to detention camps. One of my Japanese girl friends in my graduating class at Renton High, an excellent student, was chosen to work in an office and was not interned. All of the Japanese people who farmed the small truck farms north, south and east of Seattle were removed with their families to these camps and it was a great loss to our area, and a sad day for our Japanese friends and neighbors.

Because we were now fighting on two different fronts, more men were needed than the voluntary army and the draft of single men could supply. They started to draft married men without children and then as they were needed, married men with families. Women joined the military and relieved men from safer duties so more men could go to the war zones. The entertainment industry sent their best singers, dancers and comedians to keep up the morale of our troops. The USO was formed as a place for military personnel to spend their leisure time and many a romance resulted in courtship and marriage.

Glen was shipped out of Fort Lewis by troop train to Fort Monmouth, N.J. for his basic training. It was an intense three months, with no time off. His short experience in the telephone company qualified him to be in the Signal Corps and when basic training was finished, he was immediately put on another troop train and on his way to the South Pacific via San Francisco. He had written me a letter as soon as he heard the direction he was headed and wanted me to meet him in Oakland.

I had just started a new job for the Van De Kamps Bakery in the triangle of buildings across from Nordstrom and Frederick & Nelson department stores in Seattle and was enjoying my new job. We had cute uniforms with Dutch hats and most of us were young women who attracted customers. The bakery sold yummy pastries and cakes and if one was damaged in some way it was termed spoiled and then we could eat it on our coffee break. The first day of training I dropped a large tray of cookies on the floor and we girls were forced to eat all those broken cookies. Oh, did we suffer. It was a fun place to work, but a letter from Glen changed my plans.

Chapter 11

I was in my room reading a letter from Glen when I got to the place where he said he was leaving for San Francisco and wanted to meet me in an Oakland Hotel. Screaming like a chicken with my head cut off, I ran down stairs and told mother the news.

When we calmed down, we called Daddy at work and asked him if we could drive our car to Oakland to meet Glen there. Daddy used a company car for work so he could spare the family car for us to use for the trip. My dear daddy was just as excited as we were. Of course, I could use the car but with one stipulation that I had to take mother with me. Who in the world would go on a trip like that and not bring your mother? My mother would need company so why not invite Glen's mother too? The more the merrier. So I called Glen's mother, Inez and told her the news and asked her if she could get ready quickly to drive with us to California. She said "of course" and arrangements were made to leave ASAP. Mother and I packed, got some money from the bank and we were ready in no time at all. I think Glen's dad brought Mrs. Odle over from Bellevue to our place and we left when she got there. What a breath-taking time. I get excited all over again, just remembering how within such a short time we were on the road singing, "California here we come."

This was quite a trip. We drove day and night, with mother and I taking turns driving. Roads were single lane and curved through the mountains, up hill and down again. We were on old Highway 99, always looking for the next service station to fill our car with gas or find a suitable place for us to grab a bite to eat.

The nights were black and it was scary too, as there weren't many cars on the road. Would three women in a car without even a man be safe and would the family car hold up under these road conditions?

We had no idea when Glen would be in Oakland and we drove as fast as we could. My letter from Glen had given us no particulars and we just had our own intuitions to go by. We were all scared and it was a good thing we had the Lord in our car to depend on.

As I remember, we didn't change clothes the entire trip from Renton to Oakland and on arrival we must have been a sight when we walked into that hotel. Glen was not there, so three scraggly looking women sat down on some seats and waited. I imagine the reception desk clerk wondered who these be-draggled women were.

But this was war and anything could happen. I'm sure the clerks thought maybe we were part of some secret mission. I wish I had a picture of Glen's entrance. Daddy had given me his eight MM movie camera to take pictures, but I didn't even think to use it. When Glen rushed in, he headed for me in a grand reunion.

How long we had with Glen that evening I can't remember, but we made arrangements to get together the next day in San Francisco at the Hotel Navarre where we thought we'd be staying. After leaving him in Oakland we drove over the Oakland Bay Bridge and found our hotel and checked in.

We had a frightening experience while on the bridge as we were carefully driving in very heavy traffic. The air raid signals went off along with all lights and we were caught in a standstill, in the middle of San Francisco Bay Bridge. Mother got so panicky and started to fall apart. Inez started to quietly quote psalms of confidence and it wasn't long before mother got ahold of herself. Probably, for the first time, we realized we were in the midst of a real war.

Glen and I did some very serious talking when we got together the next day. We had only a couple of days to be together as his unit was in the Presidio, the point where the troops were placed before embarking for the South Pacific.

I wanted to get married, but Glen did not. He told me he didn't want me to be married to him if he came back without a leg or some other drastic injury. I laughed, and said that it wouldn't happen, he would be all right. God would take care of him. It didn't take long for me to persuade him to marry me as we both got caught up in the excitement of the moment. Can you feel our emotions building?

Glen finally said okay he would talk to the chaplain and see how it could be arranged. He always did say I talked him into marrying me. The law in the State of California stated that there had to be a three-day waiting period between obtaining a marriage license and the actual wedding.

It was possible to go before a judge and get a wavier of the three day waiting period, however a blood test was necessary and that could not be waived. I got my blood test and stood in line in the courthouse to see a judge for the waiver. The couple in front of me finally obtained their waiver and then were married by the judge.

When it came my turn, I showed the judge my blood test and requested a waiver and he gave it to me. Then he said, "Where is the young man?" I said, "In the Presidio, we're going to get married in a church." Surprised, the judge had expected to marry us right then.

On my way back to the hotel, I met our Pastor Bill McNutt's sister Bea and her husband on the street. Can you imagine God's timing and the impossibility of us meeting in such a huge city as San Francisco? I told her I was getting married the next day and wanted her to stand up with me. She was delighted to be part of our wedding. The place where we would be married was Glad Tidings Bible Institute, a Christian school in downtown San Francisco.

Meanwhile, Glen was in the Presidio trying to get someone to find a valid blood test in his file to use. But the person going through his records for the test turned the page showing where Glen was being sent and Glen saw he was going to Honolulu. He would be stationed in the Signal Center in an underground location at Tripler General Hospital. What a relief for him to know his destination and the type of duty he would have.

I made arrangements with Rev. Keys to marry us and he said he would be happy to. I had worked it all out. Just the way I did everything. I hadn't even stopped to pray and ask God what He thought. That was my way of doing things. Something so serious as marriage should be considered carefully to have God's approval, but I was in such a tizzy I didn't even take time to pray. It took me many years to learn to go to the Lord in prayer before I made a serious decision.

The day we were married was windy, as was usual for San Francisco. I got my hair fixed in a beauty parlor and wore my old, light blue suit with a new white blouse. It didn't take long for the wind in San Francisco to do a number on my hair. This was before the days of good hair spray that would keep your hair set in place. We used sugar water or thick setting lotion to set a pin curl and when you combed it out you never knew how long it would stay that way.

I looked for a flower vendor on the street and purchased three small corsages of pink and yellow roses for my mother, Inez and me to wear. I should have remembered to get Bea, the gal who was standing up as my witness, a corsage too, but I wasn't thinking clearly.

When we were all ready, we drove to the Presidio to pick up Glen. He was all slicked up. Someone had loaned him a belt that was worn over his uniform jacket that had a strap over one shoulder as well as around his waist. He looked handsome. We drove to Glad Tidings Bible Institute and found our way through the sanctuary to the pastor's study. Bea McNutt and her husband were already there as well as Pastor Keys. A girl who was practicing on the organ provided the background music for our ceremony.

In introducing Bea to Mrs. Odle, I got their names mixed up and started to get the giggles. From then on my nerves were expressed by fits of laughter. I don't know where Glen got the little wedding band we used temporarily until we could get a regular wedding ring, but it served the purpose. I wasn't married because I had a ring on my finger, but because I gave my heart and life over to Glen and we became one.

Both of us had very little money in our pockets and we gave the minister what we could and what we had left we intended to use for our wedding supper. Can you imagine getting married without a little nest egg hidden away somewhere on us? No fancy expensive wedding for us, just a quick ceremony before Glen left for the South Pacific and then I would go home to work at Boeing. Through the years I regretted not having a wedding with family and friends in attendance, but when I tell about our wedding it usually wins the prize for being the most different.

After our marriage, we went out to Golden Gate Park and the rhododendrons and other flowering shrubs were blooming beautifully. Mother took some pictures of us standing in the flowers and I remember I felt like all the festivities were happening to someone else. The pictures we took of us together in the park are someplace with the other eight MM movies we took on Daddy's camera while we were in San Francisco.

After our time in the park, Mother and Mrs. Odle drove out to the Fremont District to see the Grays, friends the folks knew when we lived in the area some 13 years earlier. Glen and I went to celebrate our wedding dinner in a chain restaurant named "The Ducky" or something like that, and our meal consisted of a hamburger and a milk shake.

I was so strung out from all that had happened since leaving Renton a couple of days before that I got sick to my stomach and thought I was going to upchuck. We had to leave our food right there on the table and go to our hotel room. Can you imagine me sick at the most romantic time in a girl's life? Glen was so thoughtful and loving and my nerves calmed as he told me he loved me and was so happy to have me as his bride.

Sometime in the middle of the night our sleep was interrupted by the phone ringing and mother asking me if I was "Mrs. Odle"? I said, "I guess so." Then Mother's response brought me back to reality. "Well we're here in the hotel lobby and we want to go to bed." We got up and dressed and the four of us took Glen back to the Presidio. Glen had two passes of four hours each, which meant he could be gone for eight hours. Those in charge had given one pass to him and a sympathetic friend had sacrificed the other one. Glen had been gone longer than eight hours so he couldn't go in the front door and had to find an unlocked window to crawl in. That was the last time I saw my new husband for nine months.

My two mothers and I left the next morning for home and work at Boeing, but "lucky Glen" left for our honeymoon on a troop ship to

Honolulu. This time we drove a more leisurely way home by going up Highway 1, the Coast Highway. It was a beautiful trip. The hillsides were covered with wild azaleas. It was spring, the time of the wild flowers' blooming, and we parked the car and walked up the slope as far as we could go. Looking out to the ocean the sky above was crystal blue. How exhilarating to breathe in the gusty wind while enjoying a sight that could last a lifetime.

When we reached the forest of redwood trees, we decided to find a nice place to stay. Cabins were few and far between and it was dark before we found a gas station with small cabins behind it. We tried to order something to eat in their small diner, but they were all out of food, so the lady warmed up some canned Campbell's tomato soup. How nice and hot it tasted to us after such a long day driving. Letting our hair down we had a good time that night.

Mrs. Odle was so much fun. She loved to quote poetry and had done so on the trip whenever she felt things were getting a little tense. But that night the poems were light and beautiful. In the morning we laughed so hard as Mrs. Odle had to have help from mother to get her undergarments on. I don't remember what kind they were, but I know it was a chore mother was not used to doing. All in all, we had an uneventful trip home. No flat tires, we didn't run out of gas or have a wreck. We just merrily rolled along through hill and dale until we got to Renton and home sweet home.

I reported to work the next Monday at Boeing and the girls all gathered around me and wanted to know what it was like to be married. I didn't know either as we were together only one night and then it was on the road again. You don't ask the kids today if they're married, you ask them how long they've been together. They buy a home, have a baby and then they have a big expensive wedding that puts them in debt for a long, long time. Some things are a little mixed up I'm afraid.

Chapter 12

Doris Johnson, my friend from Boeing, and I grew very close. Besides sharing work space every day, I visited her in her apartment in Seattle many times. One time we took some sexy pictures with just our bras and panties on to send to our lovers and these pictures went through the war with them. Her boyfriend Rollin Michelsen was finishing his college teaching certificate and would soon be a math teacher. But the draft got him too. When she got word that he was going to basic training, she flew home to be with him before he left.

Rollin was going by train to his destination in Oklahoma City. He was to be instructed on how to map out from the air the areas in Italy where the troops would be going. Doris got on the train in North Dakota to be with him before he left, just to say goodbye, and she decided to go with him. What a crazy stunt for her to do, but Doris was like that. Impulsive. When they got to Oklahoma City, they stayed in a hotel that night and the next day went to a minister's home and were married. After Rollin shipped out, she stayed there in the city for quite a long time, working in a very good job.

Meanwhile, I was working seven days a week at Boeing with little time off. Such long hours began to be a drag on me. To get away from the job, at lunch I would take my sack lunch to Rhodes Department Store across the street from the McDermott Building, where I worked, to listen to the music being played on a huge pipe organ. Some days I would go to the Bon Marche and watch the oriental girls fix runs in women's silk hose or just shop around looking for new hose in different stores. Hose were very expensive and when we got a run or a hole, we'd have them professionally repaired by these women.

I was still living with the folks, which was a long bus ride home at night from work in downtown Seattle to Renton and up the Benson Highway, six miles to the folks' place. Day after day was too much for anybody to keep up both body and spirits.

We had to have a medical examination to get a job at Boeing, to be sure we weren't pregnant and they required a doctor's certificate stating a medical problem in order to leave your job. Yes, I'm telling the truth every single young woman had to have these examinations. Finally, my doctor gave me a qualifying statement to leave and I was out of there. It seemed more logical for me to get another less demanding job right in Renton, working for the government than making that trip each day.

I applied for a job working for the Housing Authority. All you had to do was fill in an application and if you could count to ten forward and back again you were hired. They were desperate for women workers.

Meanwhile, I wrote Glen faithfully and he responded when he found time. He was attached to the 9th Signal Service Company situated underground on the property of Tripler General Hospital in Honolulu, testing lines and cables for the island of Oahu. His work schedule was ideal for sight seeing and his time at war was easy compared to most other soldiers. He was having a good time there playing handball, swimming, and one time he had tried riding the waves at Waikiki Beach and got a terrible sunburn on the back of his legs.

I received word from a mutual friend that he had met Glen and spent some time with him. The person also said Glen went to the show with him and I was really upset about that. You see, at that time our church was so strict they thought going to shows was really sinful. My next letter to Glen was not at all kind. He responded by sending me a dozen red roses in the mail. What a great way for him to put out my fire. Now you know the folks lived on a rural route and I don't know how many days it took to get the flowers to our mailbox. They were in bad shape when I got them and I was so ashamed of myself when I looked at those wilted roses.

For nine long months I worked, wrote Glen letters, listened to war news and tried to keep a happy face. Glen had very little news to tell in his letters, but he did say there was a possibility he could qualify for Officers Candidate School and if so, he wanted me to meet him in San Francisco. One day in February, when I got a letter that he had been approved for the school, I realized this meant he was on his way. You see all his letters were censored and if there was any information in them regarding the war, that area was cut out. (Loose lips sink ships.) Movement of men would mean a troop ship was on the way. By the way, I didn't mention their time on a troop ship was pretty unbearable. Some of the ships were not military and they were jammed in staterooms with all their gear. When the weather was rough, it was not unusual for men to get sick and then they threw their soiled clothes overboard. The trips were rough and hazardous, with enemy submarines hunting for them in their shipping lanes. The letter I got was the one I had been waiting for, that told me Glen was on the way home. I was so fortunate the censor had not cut out the portion regarding Officer Candidates School and I had to get going to California again.

I was on my way to California, this time alone. The train station in Seattle was filled with people going and coming every which way and standing in long lines. They pushed and shoved as you tried to board the cars, with no seat assignments, just first come, first served. There weren't enough seats on the train for the number of tickets sold and if you didn't have a seat you had to stand in the isle or sit on your luggage there. The dining cars had been removed from the trains, so when they made a stop to get water etc. you were allowed off the train, where people had food stands set up to meet the needs of the people.

Whenever we passed a train, I stretched my head to see if Glen was on the passing train. I arrived in San Francisco and made my way to Hotel Navarre. To my chagrin the hotel had been turned into a "serviceman only" hotel. Our plans were to meet there, so what was I to do now? I had to find a room and the fellow at the front desk directed me to another hotel close by. I told him I was expecting my husband and would he please direct him to the St. Francis Hotel when he came.

In the hotel, my waiting game began. Every so often, I would go to Hotel Navarre and ask if Glen had come yet. The answer was always no.

I waited a couple of days and was scared to death that I had missed Glen. I kept praying that he would find me. Without warning he came busting into my room and we were together again. Can you imagine two people looking and finding each other in such a large city as San Francisco? We went out to Golden Gate Park and walked so happy and carefree. Glen said he had gone to the hotel Navarre only to be told no women were registered. He went back again later and the fellow was on duty that I had given the message to was there. Glen said that if he hadn't gotten that message then he would have taken the next train to Seattle. Thank the Lord he got the message and I wasn't left there alone.

Everyone at home was happy to see Glen when we got there. He had been given a short leave to spend with his family before leaving for Officer Candidate School in Red Bank, N.J. For an outing, both families took their cars on a trip to Mt. Rainier for a picnic. Glen's dad had it all figured out how long it would take us to get to the lodge and at every stop he wanted us to hurry so that his time schedule wouldn't be off. Who cared about the scenery, we had to get to the picnic area and back on time.

Chapter 13

I made arrangements to go with Glen back to New Jersey and purchased a ticket on the same train Glen was on. Grandma LaDuke packed a shopping bag full of good food for us to take. Glen surprised me with a beautiful orchid corsage to wear and I wore them with a cotton dress and a navy blue hat. Women wore hats for most occasions and this was a very important one for me. We were leaving to begin our life together in that big world out there. Did I have enough money for such an adventure? I'm sure I didn't care about or think that far ahead. I could always find a job wherever we went.

This was a regular train and as usual, it was packed. At every station, people either got on or off. When we encountered a troop train, our train would pull off on the sidetracks and wait for the troop train or trains to pass. What a slow trip across country it was. We played little finger games, slept and snuggled up together in our seat. Every stop the red cap would ask me if I wanted to be brushed off. You see it was their duty when a person would get off the train, he took a little brush and tidied them up. Everyone was looking for something to do. Once a guy in the seat across from us asked as we sat up straight, "Who won the match?" Guess he thought we were wrestling. We had plenty to eat, thanks to grandma. She had packed that sack with fried chicken, sandwiches, fruit and desserts and we shared it with those around us. Bless her heart. She was a thoughtful one.

On our train there were only a few Pullman cars where the seats made up into bunks and Glen, because he was traveling on Army orders, had a top bunk for "one person". At night when all were safely tucked in their bunks by the porter, I crawled up in Glen's bunk and slept with him. We did this all across the country without the porter knowing it until we got on the Pennsylvania RR. That guy was a little too smart for us. Checking the bunks he put his hand inside our bunk and caught us, bare-naked. He raised a rumpus and called the conductor, who made Glen pay for me to use the bunk with him the rest of the way. The porter must have kept an eye on where I was sitting during the day and when I was not there at night, knew I was in a bunk some place.

As we got closer to our destination I began to get worried about where I would stay in Red Bank, New Jersey. I met a young lady on the train who lived there and she said there was a nice hotel that let Army wives rent rooms and possibly I could get one. I was sure the problem was solved. When we arrived in New Jersey we went to the hotel and I tried to check in. The girl at the desk was so sorry they were completely full. However she took pity on me and told me the lady she stayed with just had an opening and gave me her address. We took a taxi to Mrs. McAloon's house and found her to be a sweet little white-haired, Irish lady. The large vacant room had twin beds and plenty of room for us, when Glen could get several days off. Front windows that looked outward to the street made the room very desirable. However, she had lots of rules that I had to abide by, but it didn't take me long before I was living in the whole house like I was their long lost granddaughter. I was given a place for my food in the refrigerator and when I got up in the morning she had squeezed my oranges and had my juice all ready for me. Her dear, little bald-headed husband was so round and jolly. He wanted me to lay my head on his lap whenever we sat on the couch. That didn't last long however after he tried to put an innocent kiss on my face.

I heard of a job in a bank and applied. I would be working with checks arriving in the bank each day and filing them in the proper place. Simple work. Everything was done by hand except they did have typewriters and adding machines. One day an infestation of termites came out of the vault, crawling slowly up the steps just like an army into the main part of the bank. They had to close the bank and get exterminators to come and take care of them. My salary was the huge sum of $14.60 a week and I was glad to get that.

Meanwhile, Glen had checked into Fort Monmouth and immediately they were into 90 days of intense training. I couldn't contact him, but I did go out to the Fort to catch a glimpse of him running from class to class with all his fellow candidates. Although, if he could see me looking for him, he had to act like he didn't. Every night the applicants were given "Plans of the Day" that told them everything they were expected to do the following day, even to the type of clothing to wear. If the orders said it would rain and for them to put on rain gear they had to put it on, even if the sun was shining and it was hot.

When Glen drew near the end of his officer's course, he was given several trip passes to go into town to be measured for his officer uniforms. They were issued all new clothes, shirts, jackets, slacks, etc. On one of his trips to town he was given an overnight pass. How lucky could we get? That night, we were asleep in one of the twin beds and I woke up to the sound of someone opening the window. My room, being in the front of the house, had two windows that opened out on to the porch roof over the front entrance. Sure enough, there was a man trying to get in my window. I jumped out of bed and ran to the window where he was and told him he couldn't come in. He said in a low voice "Take it easy, take it easy." I called Glen a couple of times but he was dead tired and fast asleep. An earthquake couldn't wake him. The guy evidently saw Glen but came ahead anyway and walked through my room out into the hall and down and stairs and out of the house. I was scared to death and Glen never even knew what was happening. On a table in front of those windows was my Bible with $200.00 in it and I was afraid the guy would get my money. He evidently wasn't a robber, but someone who had seen me coming and going and had come for something other than money. I was concerned about my money and didn't even think the guy might hurt me. Thank the Lord, Glen was there, even if he was fast asleep. Now, where did I get all that money?

I heard that there were openings at the base and took the bus out to the Employment Office and was immediately given a job in the Provost Marshall's Office. It was my first experience of working around soldiers and I had to be on my guard all the time. They thought I was there for their enjoyment. I did typing, took dictation, filing, routing mail and greeting visitors, some who were happy and free and others who were in hand-cuffs and unhappy. My salary jumped to $30.00 a week, more than twice what I was getting at the bank. And then being on base, I could see Glen more after work when the soldiers marched on the parade ground. To see the entire group as they marched during an official parade in the field was spectacular. However, my eyes were mostly searching for only one person, my special soldier.

To get to the base, I walked to the train station where commuters had their breakfast of muffins and coffee at a small café. Seats were nonexistent at a walkup counter and you had to stand and yell your order over the heads of a milling crowd and eat anyplace you could. My bus destination was Fort Monmouth base, while others ran to the train and pushed to board a seat to New York. Think of this routine every day on your way to work?

The daily news on the base reported the candidates who had washed out and those still in school. Finally, the day came when those who had successfully finished the course assembled around the flagpole, and my husband was among those celebrating. There was a brief ceremony and when the successful were declared 2nd Lieutenants, those new hats flew up in the air with a shout and the audience and graduates became one. Another class now wore medals, received a week's pass and their first pay as a lieutenant.

I had made arrangements for us for a short stay at Big Moose Lodge in upper New York State and we traveled by train, first to tour a little of New York City, the Empire State Building and the attractions at Radio City. When we got to our destination, we were surprised we were the only occupants in that beautiful Lodge. It didn't take us long to figure out why. It was deer fly season and the little buggers made a beeline to anything resembling hair and bit like fire. The part in my hair was a bloody mess. When we went outside I had to wear a towel over my head to keep them off. Glen wore his hat outside and in to protect his head.

We had the pick of the best table in the dining room and our server gave us special service, as we were the only couple there. We spent a lot of time in our room and Glen had fun trying on his new wardrobe and modeling it for me. When we went swimming we had to run and get in the water and stay below the surface to escape the flies dive-bombing us. They tried to ruin our time there at Big Moose Lodge, but we wouldn't let them.

The scenery was beautiful and the lodge lovely. We took a canoe and paddled across the lake. In the middle we got hung up on a rock and thought we were going to wreck the canoe getting off of it. A wind with rain came up though and stirred up the waves and we were able to paddle off of it. At the closest shore, we took refuge from the pounding rain under our overturned canoe. It seemed as though everything was trying to spoil our time there, but love overshadowed every attempt. Our vacation was far too short, but it did enable Glen to rest after that 90 days of running and pressure before it was back to the troops and then on to Europe.

When we got back to Fort Monmouth, Glen was dispatched to a battalion in the Army Engineers because there was a surplus of Signal Corps Officers. His first place of duty was at Fort Belvoir, VA just outside of Alexandria, VA. As I still had a commitment to my job at the Provost Marshall's Office, I remained at Red Bank, N. J. Near the end of my time there, I got sick and had a stay in Ft. Monmouth hospital. I was pregnant. I had been to the army doctor and on my way out of the building fainted. A soldier carried me in and I was admitted immediately to the hospital. The room I was put in was one long ward with bed after bed of either army women or soldiers wives who were in for various problems. Because I was miscarrying, they rushed me in to surgery and gave me a D & C. They discussed whether to give me a blood transfusion or not, and decided against it. Using hindsight, I am so glad they didn't because I have negative blood and that type of blood hadn't yet been discovered. If they had given me positive blood, I would have had serious consequences. God was watching over us.

When it was time for me to come home from the hospital, Glen got a weekend pass from Belvoir and after picking up my things at the apartment, we went south of Fort Monmouth by train to Ft. Belvoir. I remember I had to ride in the last car of the train where I could get as much fresh air as possible and rode with my head between my knees. I was so woozy and sick. When we got to Washington, DC we took a taxi to a hotel in Alexandria, VA and Glen left me there to go back to the base.

At night the floor was crawling with cockroaches and I was afraid to put my feet down. Oh, for some way to get out of that place. I saw a small card on the hotel's bulletin board of an available room in a private home in the area, and as soon as I was strong enough I went to investigate.

This home was truly unique. Three stories tall, each house touching one house on one side, with a narrow ally on the other side. There was no front yard, you just stepped from the sidewalk onto the front steps. No need for the landlady to have a lawn mower as she didn't have a lawn. The lady who owned the house was a tall good-looking woman who, when in her prime, was a reporter for a newspaper in Washington, DC. She took me up to a back bedroom on the third floor. It had a screened-in porch in back where you could look into her small backyard. She had one plum tree in her yard and you would have thought she had an orchard full of plum trees, the way she talked. She made damson plum preserves she was so proud of and rightly so, as they were truly delicious. My room was lovely and perfect for me. She rented it to me on a weekly basis, as we didn't know how long I would be there.

She was so good to me and treated me like her own daughter. I was fortunate because I wasn't at all well. But God was taking care of me by putting me with that wonderful, compassionate woman. I had no place to cook meals, so that meant going to a restaurant nearby to eat. I met other young women whose husbands were also at Fort Belvoir and we made arrangements to meet and eat together. I lost a lot of weight and my skirts began to look like I was wearing someone else's wardrobe.

One morning I awoke to severe vertigo and the lady called her doctor. He came and gave me some medicine and instructed her to keep me in bed that day. She put me in her own bed and watched over me like my mother would have. How fortunate I was to be with her. I don't understand why this happened to me, but I know each difficulty I had when I was following Glen around the country made me more dependent upon the Lord. When we left I don't remember paying my doctor's bill or what I owed her. I sure hope we paid all our bills.

Glen was attached to an Army Engineers' Battalion that was shipping out and he arranged a ride for us to Missouri with another officer and his wife. I didn't know these people and here I was sick and causing them all this trouble. I rode in the back seat of their car with my head in Glen's lap most of the trip. It was most embarrassing. When you have vertigo you have trouble standing and walking and your sight is affected. Reaching Missouri, we found that there was only one hotel in Neosho, the nearest town to Glen's next place of duty, and it was full. Both of us women had to find places to stay, so we drove about 30 miles north, to find another hotel in Joplin, MO where we could stay a few days.

When my time was up in the hotel, I took my luggage and rode the bus to Neosho, MO to try to get in the hotel there. Fortunately, they had a room but only for several days. Now I had to find a place to live or be out on the street. I was still feeling punk most of the time, but knowing my stay in the hotel was limited, I walked along the street silently praying for direction. I stopped where a church was on one corner and the other three corners had homes. Which home should I try? I felt directed to go to one place and made my way up the steps and rang the bell. An older lady answered and I told her my plight. She took me in and upstairs to a nice room with an iron posted bed, with a few furnishings. This was another of God's answers to my prayers.

The other bedroom she was renting to another army wife from the South and we became friends. I found out she was a Christian girl and she directed me to a Methodist church that ministered to wives, by providing a place of refuge. They had crafts and fun things to do to help pass the lonely days without our friends and husbands. I made several wooden articles that I am proud to still have. One is a nine by twelve inch tray that I painted flowers on and have used all these years, and the other a small long box to put gloves in that I made for my mother. On the back of the box I wrote the following.

"Made by Shirley in 1943 Neosho, MO, for my mother Hazel Cross." Glen was just out of OCS and assigned to a combat battalion before going to Europe.

I knew no local people in this small, quaint country town. It had a town square in the middle with a few businesses around the square and behind the businesses were quaint old homes. Several restaurants, a few churches, a drug store etc. made up the places I can remember. I ate in one restaurant there and became friends with a few army wives who were in the same predicament as I was. Most officer wives were better off, as we had money for our food, but I don't know how the enlisted wives existed. I remember one girl who ate breakfast where I did, who had hardly any money at all. The waitress would ask her what she wanted and she always chose the cheapest thing on the menu. Then the waitress would bring her a nice meal and write down and charged her for the cheap one she had ordered. Not honest, but I believe it saved many a young girl. I wonder if the owner realized our waitress was doing that? Probably.

Neosho was full of homes where young women were accommodated. A young girl told me she slept in an attic room with beds along the wall, that had just a curtain separating each bed. No privacy at all, and this room was full to capacity most of the time. Imagine what it was like to have your husband come to visit in a place like that?

I continued to look for a place where Glen could come if he had a day off and the Lord answered that prayer too. The answer came in a nice ground floor apartment in a house in the newer part of town. The owners had divided the house in two parts and made the front room into a bedroom. The kitchen was on the same side of the house, with the full bath there too. I was really comfortable and Glen could stay with me, without going through someone else's front room. It is amazing how God provided for us. One night, Glen had a pass and was able to stay with me, but the next morning when he got up he had come down with a fever and cough. We called the base and told them he was sick. Thinking they'd let him stay there with me, I put my pink bed jacket on him and tucked him into our nice warm bed. It wasn't long before the doorbell rang and when I opened it, there were the corps men to pick up Glen to take him to the infirmary. They asked him if he had called them and Glen shouted, "Blank No". Was he ever embarrassed to have them see him in my bed jacket.

I kept in contact with Doris Michelsen, as she had remained at her job in Oklahoma City when Rollin went overseas. We made arrangements to get together and do some shopping in the city. The officers from Glen's battalion were having a ball in their club and because I didn't have a formal dress, Glen wanted me to get a pretty one for the party. I took the train south to the city and Doris met me and showed me around the department stores. If there was anyone who knew her way around all the stores, it was Doris. She was the world's best shopper. After trying on quite a few dresses, I purchased a lovely, long, black taffeta dress with brass hobnails on it. It was perfect for the ball and we enjoyed the only officer's party they had before Glen left for Europe.

On one occasion, we went up to Joplin and Glen bought a second hand Buick for us that could go like the wind. I would need transportation soon, as his battalion left for maneuvers and I planned to follow him. The tires were shot on the car and when we got home I would have to get either new or recapped tires. In fact, on the way home after buying the car we had a flat tire, and a young army enlisted man who was hitch hiking where the flat occurred, changed the tire for Glen. It was pouring rain and the poor guy got soaking wet. But he was glad to do it because Glen gave him a ride back to Neosho.

When we got home, it was my duty to get the car ready to roll, so I went to the ration board and they gave me coupons to purchase a couple of retread tires. I got the tires from a young man that lived in a gas station and was running it for someone else. His kindness made it possible for me to get gas coupons too, for my trip, so I could follow Glen's battalion.

I asked two girls to go with me for company, whose husbands were also going on maneuvers in the hills of Tennessee. When the battalion left, we followed a short distance behind, stopping and starting right behind the vehicles. One time, the convoy made a potty stop right on the road and we didn't know what to do so we passed them and there they were like soldiers on review. We continued to lead them until we got to Memphis. We left the convoy and went into town to look for lodging.

I don't know where I let the girls out on their own, but I think it was at the YWCA in Memphis, when I went into the locker room to rest and look for leads on a place for me to stay. I found an ad for a room in a private home and called to see if it was still available. It was and I drove there and rented the room. The room on the ground floor was in the back of the house, with large windows and lots of sunshine. The owners were a lady named Mrs. Bumpas and her husband, who owned an electrical store there in Memphis. The place was rather new and the lady was a typical lovely lady with a southern drawl. Her mother lived with them and she chewed snuff, which was not that unusual in the south.

Glen found me through the YWCA and he and his jeep driver drove into the backyard in a cloud of dust. Was I ever happy that they found me. He could stay only long enough to give me directions to find the headquarters for the maneuvers at an abandoned college campus. The Army Exchange store was where he wanted me to wait for him, until he was available. Looking back now, I just can't imagine the things I did, most of the time all alone and trusting only in God for my safety. I was only twenty and a young girl from a sheltered life in little old rural Renton. Now days, I wouldn't dare start out alone, with little money and not knowing where I was going. No credit cards or way to get money from the folks. I followed the army trucks, because I knew Glen was in one of them somewhere. This was mock warfare, but still very serious business. They were simulating a battle between two armies and to distinguish between these armies they wore different colored armbands. They even took prisoners. I don't know what they did at night or where they slept, but it wasn't an overnighter in a Boy Scout Camp. However, in the Army Exchange things were very normal and you wouldn't know a mock battle was going on just outside in the hills.

When the maneuvers were over, the battalion went to Fort Chaffee in Fort Smith, Arkansas to make final preparations for the real thing in Europe. Glen had permission to drive our car, with all our worldly possessions and it was so nice to let him take the responsibility and do the driving.

As we drove into the area around Fort Smith, I thought it was so beautiful, with tall poplar trees and an abundance of green shrubs and lovely homes. The weather was warm and sunny. We were fortunate to be able to rent a nice home across from a golf course that was just right for us. The homeowners also owned the golf course and let us play golf as much as we wanted. That's where Glen first taught me to play golf. I can't remember where we got the clubs to use, but probably at the clubhouse. But Glen was so happy with the arrangements and I'm sure he felt he'd died and gone to heaven.

I made friends with the two families on the dirt road facing the course. One was a nice family with several girls and the other was a couple of friendly sisters, only one of them had a husband. I never saw him, but I sure heard stories about his escapades. Their cooking style was really different from how mother taught me. They cooked things all day, boiling their meat in a big pot, with okra and other strange vegetables. The younger gal, the larger of the two, would have stomach aches and she'd lie on the floor rolling around groaning and saying she had "stomach complaint." What a sight she was.

Our house was next door to the family with two girls, the youngest about ten years old. They had huge poplar trees in their yard and when we'd have a storm, some of the branches would come down in our yard. One time, we had a really bad lightening storm and dumb me, I was ironing clothes in the dining room. At the same time, the lightening was crashing around the house. The homeowner, Mrs. Bumpas, came running over from the golf course and hollered for me to come with her, down in the storm cellar. It was some storm and when we opened up the storm door to come out, I was amazed at the destruction. Some of their trees were completely down in our yard. Many of the trees that lined the golf course were uprooted, and laying all over the fairways. Cleaning up all of those trees kept golfers from playing for many days.

Chapter 14

At the end of our street was an old-fashioned grocery store. I used to go there and get Orange Crush or Green River soft drinks. The proprietor would greet me in his southern drawl and when I'd leave he'd say, "Ya'all come back."

Mother was working at Boeing and during the summer when school was out she didn't know what to do with Bobby. He was only nine years old at the time. Someone in her acquaintance was going down South and her travel plans put her within a short distance from Fort Smith. She told mother she'd love to take Bobby with her and promised she would see personally that he was delivered to our door. It seemed to be mother's solution to where she would have Bobby for the summer. We would be happy to have Bobby with us and looked forward to the day of his arrival. Days passed, but Bobby didn't come. What had happened to that kid, mother said she had sent him?

One morning, when Glen was leaving for the fort, I told him I had a feeling that Bobby needed help. Not having any information, even what bus line they were traveling on, we could not do anything to ease my fears about my "baby brother" as I called him. That morning, I was still in bed when I heard someone out at our gate. I got up and there was a taxi driver standing beside his cab, with Bobby in hand. I ran outside so happy, as I was really concerned about him. Thank you, Lord, Bobby was safe.

The driver said he found Bobby in the bus station, with no one with him. He'd been there all night. Bobby said he had amused himself by watching the cockroaches crawl up and down the back of the person sleeping on the bench in front of him. The driver said that Bobby had told him he was going to his sister's house across from the golf course and that his sister's husband was a soldier. That's all the information the driver had to go by. No address or even which golf course.

The taxi driver proceeded to go to every golf course around Fort Smith and he couldn't find our house. He even took Bobby to a Catholic school for boys and had planned to take him back and leave him at the school, if he couldn't find us. I was so thankful to the Lord for bringing Bobby safely to us. I gave the driver a nice check and Bobby with his little suitcase, became a member of our family. Oh, by the way, mother had put a towel and soap in his suitcase along with clean underwear, but Bobby had not used the soap and towel or clean clothes on his journey. Was mother angry at her friend? We all were. It seems her friend put Bobby on the bus without directions, other than he was to get off at Fort Smith bus terminal and we would pick him up there. It was a real miracle that we ever saw Bobby again.

Bobby made himself right at home, playing in our yard and with the little girls next door. He pretended that he was in the army and swung on the fence gate door and hit the fence with a stick yelling "Hail Hitler." He was making so much noise that it caught the attention of the owner in the clubhouse, and the golfers across the street, and the owner came over and said if he didn't behave himself he would have to go home. To go home was harder than she knew. From then on I gave him jobs to do.

I was pregnant for the second time and as usual sick. The first chore I gave Bobby was to clean my floors. Now how could a little nine-year-old kid wash the kitchen floor and do a good job? Well he tried. One day, in answer to his call, I came into the kitchen and found the kitchen floor flooded with soapy water. Soap was not only on the floor, but the mopboards. Soap, soap everywhere, and he couldn't get it up. I wonder why he didn't pretend he was playing hockey and have some fun? He could push the vacuum cleaner though and did other little jobs I gave him. He made a game out of everything and you could easily hear him, yelling and having fun slaying dragons.

Glen took him riding horses one day and Bobby was all talk about how he would handle the horse, until he got on the gentlest nag they had. He cried so hard, Glen had to take him off. Glen was really disgusted with him as that was the end of Glen's ride too. Glen was learning that fatherhood was harder than he thought.

One evening, Glen brought home one of his officer friends for dinner and after we had eaten, the fellows said there was a carnival in town and wondered if I wanted to go with them. Of course I wanted to go. My days and nights were mostly spending my time at home and to get out and see things was a great opportunity. This was just a small carnival with barkers and people selling ointments, cotton candy and various freak shows, like a two-headed snake or sisters joined at the hip. Nothing like the fairs and carnivals we had in our town. There was one show that the fellows were interested in and being men you can understand. It was exotic dancers whose costumes were brief, and I mean brief. I went into the tent with the guys and I didn't see another woman, except the ones performing. I stayed close to Glen, for fear I'd have to do my act alone that Margie and I did for Grandma LaDuke. "I'm just a sailor from across the sea come to see if you'll marry me."

Several days later, after Glen had gone to the base, I got out of bed and went into the bathroom and a tiny completely formed baby fell into the commode. I was heartsick. I had that mothering desire deep inside and I so wanted us to have a family to love and raise for the Lord. The fetus was about two or three inches long and you could see the little head and knees tucked up. I didn't know what to do with it, so I disposed of it. I was so upset and felt so alone, with no one with me who understood. This was the second baby I had lost. I never forgot that baby, as I had actually held it in my hands and examined it. I'm sure I'll see that little one someday in heaven. I was deeply touched by that experience. Somehow, I think it was a boy.

Glen was given a furlough for the last time, before being sent to England and we took Bobby home with us. Those were difficult times. Loved ones not wanting to say goodbye, and friends coming to wish you well with the future so uncertain.

Only God knew the future and the plans He had for us. All we could do was put our lives in his hands and trust Him.

Phil had been drafted into the infantry and after his basic training, he was sent to the East Coast before going by troop ship to Europe. Marge took the same train we took on our way back to Neosho, on her way to New Jersey to be with Phil, until he left. We were with Marge until we got to the junction where our train went south to Fort Smith and Margie's, East to New Jersey. After Marge said her goodbye to Phil, she took a train down to our place to stay with me until Glen left and we drove our car home.

It was a sad day when Glen's battalion left on the troop train, with hundreds of soldiers and their wives tearfully clinging to each other. Officers were giving directions, trying to hurry the loading of the cars. Of course, we were a part of this bitter event. Marge and I had gone to see Glen before he left and it took some doing to find him. I remember how awful I felt, when I gave Glen his last kiss and he walked away without looking back. I would be going home to work, family and friends but he had no idea what to expect or what his chances were to be home again. He kept a straight face and said his goodbye, like a real soldier. I didn't realize then, but I do now, how courageously he faced his future.

Marge and I were both pregnant again and plans were to go home to Washington as soon as we could pack our things and clean up the house before leaving in the big Buick. I am so glad that we had that car. The interior was spacious and the trunk huge, with all our things fitting comfortably inside. We felt safe in our car and trusted that God would guide us from Missouri to Washington, protected from harm.

Everyone had a suggestion as to which way we should travel and exactly which highway we took, I can't remember. I do know we got a map and drove north through Kansas and into Colorado. So far, it was relatively flat. As we approached the city of Pueblo, they were harvesting fields of onions and the smell was so strong, it reminded me of pickle making time. We got us a room in a hotel there and as soon as we got in our room, we had a telephone call from a couple of fellows who wanted us to come to their room for refreshments. We told them we were both married and not interested. They called several more times before they gave up.

The next day our car just purred around corners in the mountains and had no trouble climbing the steep hills around Colorado Springs. When we entered the city, I told Margie something was wrong with my steering wheel and thought I should drive into the next service station. I told the attendant how the steering wheel wobbled in my hands during the curves and he said he would see what he could do. He got in the car and grabbed the wheel with both hands and the wheel came off. A loving Lord had once more saved us from disaster.

After the steering wheel was fixed, we drove on to Denver, where Aunt Ella Swan lived. She had married Oscar Swan, Grandma LaDuke's brother. We stayed a few days with her and Marge and I did a little sightseeing. Everywhere we went we were reminded of our husbands and the uncertainty of life. In one department store we visited, they were showing a moving picture of troops in battle and men getting killed and injured and we just couldn't take it. We got out of there as soon as we could and put all those thoughts out of our minds of death and war.

We drove on to Salt Lake City and some place on the highway, leaving the city, we saw a young soldier hitchhiking. We stopped and picked him up and found that he was going to Fort Lewis. He was a nice guy and because our gas ration coupons were nearly gone, we stopped at a ration board and he showed them his leave papers and we were able to get enough gas coupons for the rest of our trip. What would we have done without help from that young man? When we got to Yakima, he left us to hitchhike on to Fort Lewis, as his leave was over the next morning. Margie got a letter from him, when we got home, thanking us and saying he got back to Fort Lewis right on time.

We arrived at Marge and Phil's house on Othello St. in Seattle and decided it would be best if we lived together, there. Philip Jr. was a couple of years old and I spent hours with him sitting on my bed, while I read to him. I helped him memorize little nursery rhymes and we developed a close bond and had a lot of fun together.

I had a specialist, who prescribed bed rest to keep me from losing our baby. Also, Margie learned how to give me a shot in the leg everyday of a new drug that was to keep me from having premature labor pains. Margie's due date was several months ahead of mine and Leann was born on March 12, 1945.

She was a darling baby, with dark hair, sparkly eyes and a sweet smile. Now they had their family, but what about ours?

I wasn't doing so well, and in April, two months before my due date, Steven Albert was born. He weighed 1 pound 10 ounces. He had difficulty breathing and they didn't have the technology in those days to help him that they do now. Several days after he was born, the young nurse who took care of him, rushed into my room and announced that he had just died. What a shock. I had already sent a telegram to Europe, telling Glen of Steven's birth and now I had to send the second telegram, with the news of our baby's death. Glen told me in a letter that the second telegram arrived before the first, so his death wasn't such a shock to him. The news of Steven's birth and death didn't seem to bother Glen too much. He had a war on his hands and getting it over with and home again was what he was concentrating on.

Mother was no longer working, so she was able to take care of getting a little casket for Steven and our church had a small service at the gravesite for him. He was buried in the Kent Cemetery near the grave of Grandma LaDuke. When mother came to the hospital to take me home, I was so weak after a week of being in bed. They placed me in a wheelchair and as I was checking out, a young nurse came running to me and said she couldn't find my baby. I had to tell her my baby had died. How difficult it was for me to leave the hospital without him. Every place I went, women had their babies and I spent a lot of time crying. Even in church, I could hardly stand it when a new baby was dedicated to the Lord or the birth of a baby was announced.

Glen's battalion was sent to England to prepare for entrance into France and Germany. They were stationed at Weston Super Mare, where Glen made friends with a family who treated him like part of their family. The wife sent me several letters and I wrote to her. Meanwhile, when Glen's troops were sent to Europe they were assigned to the 3rd Army, commanded by General George Patton. Because the war was nearly over, the action Glen's battalion saw was the roads they repaired and the bridges they built.

The U.S. and Allied Forces invaded Europe at Normandy, France on "D" Day June 6th 1944 in the greatest amphibious landing in history. In the Battle of the Bulge, the Nazis failed in their counter offensive in January 1945 and Adolf Hitler committed suicide in his mountain retreat, on April 30, 1945. Meanwhile, President Franklin Roosevelt was just into his fourth term as president when he died in Warm Springs, GA on April 12, 1945 (just eight days before Steven was born). Vice President Harry S. Truman became our president. The war became intense with our forces in the South Pacific and in Europe having heavy casualties. Marines landed on Iwo Jima and took control of the island and US Forces invaded Okinawa and captured the island in June, 1945.

Germany surrendered on May 7, 1945 and May 8, 1945 was proclaimed V-E Day. The war was still raging in the South Pacific and the first atomic bomb was dropped on Hiroshima on Aug. 8, 1945 killing about 75,000 people and on Aug. 9, 1945 the second bomb was dropped on Nagasaki killing about 40,000 people and Japan agreed to surrender Aug.14, 1945, formally on Sept 2, 1945.

Glen was on a ship to the South Pacific when the war with Japan was over and his ship changed direction and landed in New Port News, VA. He was sent to Fort Lewis and the family went to get him there. Glen and I stayed at my folks place and he called into his battalion headquarters everyday until he was separated from the service on Feb. 8, 1946. Home at last. Not even the most lucrative offer to stay in the service or to be a part of the National Guard could entice him. He would have nothing to do with the service. He was a civilian now and wanted to put thoughts of his four years away from home and in the service behind him.

Chapter 15

"Give thanks to the Lord Almighty, for the Lord is good, His love endures forever."

Jeremiah: 33:11

This was the first day of the rest of our lives together. Could we put behind us four years of loneliness, fears, pain and uncertainty, and begin to live normal lives again? We were carrying baggage that should be sorted out, dealt with, forgiven and forgotten. Where were the lovers who were at that train station in Fort Smith over a year before? Would God heal those shattered hearts and make them one again? I'm sure He was willing but would we cooperate?

Glen started back to work at the telephone company in the Seattle-Rainier office and we lived with my folks at their ten acres until we could make other arrangements. I was not working then, just staying home and trying to be a housewife and enjoying Glen's companionship again. I was kept busy with a lot of washing and ironing of the dirty clothes Glen had collected during his last few weeks of travel to get home. In my mind's eye I see that pile of several large duffle bags of clothes to be sorted and washed. What a job I had before me. Besides the dirty clothes he had a bag of the spoils of war from his last tour of duty in Germany.

One of the bags held an unusual assortment of articles his men had found in a cave intended for Nazi troop use. Defeated in war and left for the taking, these brand new articles such as fur-lined boots and overalls, heavy jackets, uniforms, some dental tools, and small personal articles were left in the cave after the troop's hasty retreat. Not knowing what to do with these articles we took them to our J. C. Penney Store in Renton and asked the manager if he would like to display the paraphernalia. He was thrilled and made a nice display in the store's front display window. Later when I got the things home again I made a pair of cowboy chaps from some fur-lined overalls for Philip Jr. to wear. He was a real cowboy now. I don't remember what we did with most of the clothes that were left. However, the dental tools were given to Glen's brother Willard who was a dentist in Seattle and years later when we had a garage sale, the fur lined Nazi boots were purchased by Bill Morris Sr., Cindy's father-in-law.

We found an upstairs apartment in the Cedar River Park Development and moved from the folks' place. These apartments had been quickly built during the war and they weren't much. The second floor occupants shared the stairs to get to their apartments and the bedrooms, kitchen and front room on that floor mirrored each other on both sides. Walls were just a thin piece of plywood and we could hear every word and action on either side as plainly as if there weren't walls at all. I could hear the ground floor door open and then footsteps come up the stairs and pause on the landing. Would they open my door?

When Glen worked the evening shift I was really afraid to be alone. I didn't even need to turn on my radio as I could hear the station the neighbors listened to. A telephone call startled me into jumping up to answer it, only to find it was in the neighbor's apartment.

With Glen working in the Rainier office and away so much, I found our relationship was different from what it had been when he left for war. I was still a small town girl and he was a man who had been away to war and seen the world. We had a hard time communicating and there seemed to be an unknown wedge between us that I could not figure out. We hid our problems from the family and tried to work them out by ourselves. I'm so glad we were still attending the Renton Assembly Church where our many friends and loved ones attended, as they gave me the spiritual support I needed. I was still grieving over our loss of Steven and the babies and children's events in church tore my heart out. I did a lot of crying and Glen didn't understand what was taking me so long to get over. I had been through the loss of three babies that I had so desperately wanted and I really needed his emotional help but received very little.

One Sunday night after the evening service, Glen went forward and knelt at the altar to seek God's help for our reconciliation. I joined him and together we prayed for forgiveness, renewal and God's help in finding our strength from Him and each other. Some things between us were made right and from that time on it was an upward climb to the closeness we once knew.

I heard about a job with the War Department's Finance Office in Seattle. They needed typists to type separation checks for service men leaving the service and we thought it would be a good idea for me to get back to work instead of being home pining most of the time. I applied and was accepted. It was tedious work, sitting at a large addressograph machine, typing checks all day long. However, there was one thing I enjoyed and that was reading out loud the recipient's funny names. I wish I could remember some of those different names. I was paid $163.00 a month and we finished the job in only two months.

Another temporary job became available in an office building at the old Renton Boeing Plant working for Lyons Van & Storage. They had a contract with the War Department to recover large equipment from Alaska that had been abandoned to the elements. Their job was to recover these items from the mud in Alaska, clean them up and sell them to private firms as quickly as possible. A large number of us girls processed the paper work for the bill of sale on the equipment when they came into the warehouses at the south end of Lake Washington. It was amazing the number of large items that were recovered and sold during this time. We were probably paid minimum wage and the faster we typed the sooner we finished the job.

I started to look for a more stable job and found a job for the Renton Chamber of Commerce and the Parks Department. My time was divided between the Chamber working for Mr. Reynolds, an Easterner and The Renton Parks Department working for two different men. I was taking dictation, typing, answering two phones and running a mimeograph machine. Not all at once though. I also picked up the slack for members of the Chamber who needed help when their office workers were absent.

Mr. Reynolds knew very little about our beloved Northwest and when questions came in over the telephone he asked me to give the answer. My job there gave me lots of various business experiences although there were times when I was alone in the office with nothing to do but what I could drum up. They had a monthly Chamber luncheon and I met all of the business owners in town. My mind slowly formed a possible job I could develop that would help these businessmen on a temporary basis when they needed help. I continued to work in this job for over a year before giving my notice to my employers that I was going to start a new business.

To start this business in 1948 I rented a small office above Puget Sound Power & Light Company. I purchased a typewriter, mimeograph machine, and small card-duplicating machine and had a phone put in. I named my business The Letter Shop. The Standard Oil Owner had a small office in the building near me and had his phone line put on my phone so I could take orders from his customers. A lawyer in the building had the same phone set up and I also did quite a bit of typing for him.

During that time, Grandpa La Duke asked us if we would like to buy a piece of property on the southwest corner of his land. It was by that little stream near my dream stump where I spent so much time when I was just a little girl. His price was $500.00 for the property and we could pay, as we were able. That sounded like a great deal to us and Grandpa La Duke wrote up a contract on a piece of scratch paper. Several months later he sent us the contract marked "Paid." What a wonderful gift.

Glen planned to build a 24 by 24 foot garage to live in and then later if we liked the area where it was situated, we would build our house. The property was on a beautiful piece of land covered with fir trees and underbrush and a little creek that could at times be a raging river. It would be quite a job to clear the land for a space large enough for our little house but we were thrilled with the opportunity to have our own place. Now to have a truck to help us take down some of those trees and get on with the building of our house.

Glen received a notice from the Veterans Department of available army surplus trucks for sale. We went down to Fort Lewis Ordinance Depot and were thrilled that the price was reasonable enough so we could purchase one. That was really great timing wasn't it?

It was a sturdy pickup truck built for war. but it had one fault, it wouldn't shift into high gear. Glen put a tow rope from our Buick to the truck and towed it all the way home while I sat in the truck steering and putting the brake on when necessary. What a tense drive home I had.

As soon as we returned home we had a mechanic fix the gears for us and from then on it was full speed ahead. Glen got some dynamite and the makings to blow up stumps and the Odle Land Clearing Company was formed. Instead of cutting the trees down he put a chain around a tree and fastened the chain to the back of the truck. When he said "GO" I drove that truck as fast as I could and the tree fell with a crash on the truck. Now the roof was reinforced so it could stand the weight of the tree or I wouldn't be telling this story now. Can you believe the whole top of the truck didn't cave in? Then he cut off the stump and tree limbs and we put them on a pile to burn later. I have since wondered why I was driving the truck and not Glen?

Some of the bigger trees had to be dug out by the roots and when they did, he'd set a charge of dynamite below them and would blow them up. Boy, those roots would come out slick and fly up in the air as we ran for safety. One night, some kids got into Glen's dynamite hiding place and took everything. For a long time we worried what they might do with all that dynamite.

It took us a long time to get enough land cleared so we could have a tractor make a road down from Benson Highway and level the spot for our little house. Glen was working during the day so most of our work on the area was done after work and on weekends. Glen drew some plans and we started by measuring out the plot for our little house. By the time we got going on the house the weather turned so cold we could hardly work. So we got an old standing household oil burner from the folks to help keep our hands warm and put it inside the area where we were working. It didn't warm the area up but when we needed to thaw out our fingers it was a lifesaver. A cement truck brought the cement for the footings and as soon as the cement set we had a load of cement building blocks delivered for Glen to start the walls. Glen mixed by hand the cement that was used between the blocks and we could see at last our little house rising up from its foundation. We had only one door but plenty of windows around the structure. When Glen put the first windows in he put them in backwards and we had to take them out and turn the windows around. The outside sill would have been on the inside if he hadn't changed it. We had many a good laugh about how little we knew about building. We were beginning builders and everything we did was all just trial and error. You've heard of the house that Jack built? Well this was the little house in the woods that Glen built.

When the place was completed, it had a combination front room and kitchen on one half of the place and a bathroom, closet and bedroom on the other half. Actually it was a nice looking little place and we painted the blocks on the outside yellow and the window trim white. There wasn't room for our washing machine in the bathroom area so we put it right in the kitchen. After a lot of hard work and some help from friends our little house was finished and we were ready to move in.

On a trip to the doctor for a regular check-up I told Dr. Lombardini all about the heart ache of losing Steven and he told me there were now new medicines available. He promised that if he didn't deliver to us a live baby, we wouldn't have to pay a thing. This news gave us hope, as we were afraid we weren't meant to have children.

The next time I became pregnant the new medicines were given in shot form. If I started to have cramps I immediately went to the doctor. The shots kept me from going into labor but it didn't keep me from feeling lousy and sick to my stomach most of the time. Because I needed help, we closed up our little house in the woods and moved back in with the folks.

I still had The Letter Shop in Renton and being pregnant and sick, mother worked for me. It soon became obvious that I couldn't continue to keep the business so I put an ad in the paper to sell it. My first inquirer was a lady from Seattle who paid me cash and I was glad to have it off my hands. At first she was upset with me because when I turned it over to her she thought business would come automatically to her.

I had been hustling for my work and had the advantage of knowing almost everyone in town. When she started to get out and meet some of the employers in Renton, her business began to grow and the shop developed into a nice business for her. When I last saw the shop, she had moved it down on the street level across the corner from the Puget Sound Power and Light Company.

Glen started back to SPC to take advantage of the G.I. Bill of Rights and hoped to finish his schooling. He was taking only a few credits each quarter so it was going to take him a lot of time to finish. Meanwhile I developed toxemia and the doctor changed my diet to six cups of salt free chicken broth, six cups of fat free milk and six chocolates a day. When I ate the chocolates I took a toothpick and slowly savored each little bite. What a diet but I was in serious trouble and I had to stick to this diet or lose the baby and maybe even my own life.

With the experience mother had acquired working for me, she opened a similar shop in the Tri-Cities area in Eastern Washington and stayed there during the week and came home on the weekends. Now I needed help during the day while Glen was at work so Glen's mother came from Bellevue to stay with us until the toxemia subsided. To pass my time, I read women's magazines and poured over the recipes, like the starving person I was.

On May 19, 1949 the baby decided to come and Glen rushed me to the Renton Hospital. We named her Kathleen Elizabeth Odle and Dr. Lombardini delivered her. His promise to us was fulfilled. She was so tiny, weighing only 3 pounds 12 ounces, two months early and she came breech. During the delivery I thought the doctor was having trouble and I was sure she would not make it. I heard a loud crack and assumed the doctor had broken her back. I told the doctor I knew she was dead and he assured me she was not and that the crying I heard was hers. I told the doctor "No, that's the lady's baby in the opposite delivery room." What a joy to have the nurse show Kathy to me, a bright-eyed little pumpkin. Her head was pointed from sitting upright in the womb and I was afraid she would have a permanent disfigurement. Our pastor's wife, who was a nurse working in the hospital at the time, assured me they would rub her head back into shape. Kathy needed no oxygen and was very active, throwing her arms and legs around in her little bed. She wanted to get going. No lollygagging around for her. The nurses were thrilled with her and she took her feeding of two ounces of milk without difficulty, just sucking away on her little bottle.

After a week I was able to leave the hospital without Kathy, but we visited her every night. We were not allowed to go into the nursery or hold her, as they were especially cautious in those days. Today they would have a party and invite all the family.

It was a month before she finally weighed five pounds and was large enough to be released to go home. The nurse put her in her little nightgown, sweater and cap and wrapped her in a receiving blanket. Then she gave her to us. It was the first time we had ever held her and we were so happy to have our darling little baby at last. When we went home we were given a routine and specific orders to follow. We were to feed her two ounces of milk every two hours, two teaspoons of pureed fruit and cereal mixed once a day with a teaspoon of canned strained meat. That was all day and all night. I soon was so tired and nervous that if she burped up I would hand her to Glen. Poor Glen was nervous and tired too, but he didn't let me know it.

Everyone loved Kathy and she was so fast in her development. However, she did want me all the time and when I was away from her she cried up a storm. One time, Glen took me out to have dinner and we left Kathy with Stella and Gene Moore, dear friends of ours. Kathy cried so loud and long that she scared their cat away, never to be found again.

You might say Kathy was raised on a church pew because we took her to church when she first got home from the hospital. We put her in her basket and took her to church nearly every time it was open and her place was on the front pew where she slept through most of the services. One night, when we were going home down the incline to the door of the little house Glen built, he was carrying the basket and slipped, fell and his elbow went down hard in the basket. We both thought he'd killed her. But when we got the basket inside the house and took the receiving blanket off of her, she was sleeping away. Thank you, Jesus, for taking care of her. You must have had something wonderful for her to do in her life. I still handled Kathy with the fear that we would do something to cause her death. When she was sleeping I listened to see if she was breathing. I was on edge all the time.

Kathy was very special to the doctor, too. We gave her first photograph to the doctor and he displayed it on his office bookcase. He was just a new, young doctor and Kathy was a real trophy as one of his first successes. Rose Huber, a Swiss lady in our church, loved her too, and made over her as if she was her baby girl. She was a seamstress and made a couple of cute little dresses for Kathy. One outfit had a little plaid skirt and when I put it on her, she looked like a little miniature doll.

In January 1950, I got pregnant again and Dr. Lombardini followed the same routine he had used for Kathy. He even came out to our little house in the woods to give me a shot when I needed it. I hadn't intended to have another baby so soon after Kathy was born, but I guess the Lord had his timetable too. This pregnancy was very much the same as my other ones. One night we went to a travelogue in Seattle about a big ship on the rolling seas. I felt woozy in the theatre and when I got home that night I didn't feel at all good. In the middle of the night when I went to the bathroom I lost a lot of blood. I called the doctor the next morning and he wanted me in his office as soon as possible, as he was sure I'd lost the baby.

The next morning I was praying and felt the baby move in my womb. I was so surprised to feel her move and was so happy that she was still alive. When I got to the Doctor's office he examined me and was surprised I was still pregnant. It was back to bed for me and the old routine. Glen's mother came again to my folks' place and stayed with us off and on until the danger was over. On July 20, 1950, Nancy Jean was born headfirst, but turned around face up, which can sometimes be a problem. She weighed three pounds six ounces and had a lot of black hair on her little round head. Oh, our joy was without measure. We now had two, beautiful little girls and both of them had not needed to have oxygen.

Nancy didn't have the strength to suck from the little bottle, so they put a tube down her throat to insert her milk and some of the canned meat directly into her stomach. The doctor told us later it was that formula that kept her alive and helped her to gain her weight. She had to be revived by the nursing staff a couple of times though and God also must have had something special for her to do in life.

About the same time, our church had asked Brother and Sister Clement, former missionaries to Japan, to be our pastors. They were wonderful people and both Glen and I grew spiritually under their ministry. In a General Conference Meeting in the Seattle Center, during a call for missionaries, we responded to the call. To prepare, Glen decided to go to Northwest Bible College in addition to Seattle Pacific College where he was already attending. He took on a heavy load, working the night shift at the telephone company and attending both schools during the morning and then home to sleep. He built himself a small shed behind our house that was just big enough for his bed to fit in, so he could sleep during the day. Later on, we used this shed for storage and to put my canning in.

We were now living in the little house that Glen built and were a happy little family. Two babies, their mother and father and one dog can make a lot of commotion in a little place. Our dog Yenta, a beautiful black and white longhaired spaniel, was so happy to see me when we brought Nancy home from the hospital that she barked and barked and kept trying to get my attention. I couldn't stand the noise so Glen put her outside. What happened to her, we'll never know. We looked all over the neighborhood and never found her. At times, I got in our car and drove even as far as Skyway in Renton looking for her. It took me a long time to get over her leaving, as I felt responsible.

Kathy was walking all around at sixteen months and wanted to help me do everything. She folded diapers and did a great job for being just over a year. It didn't take long for her to start talking too and she kept up a steady stream. I had purchased a Singer sewing machine right after the war was over and I started to sew again. I made dresses for the girls of the same pattern, only different colored materials. Everyone thought the girls were twins. We got Kathy some new black patent leather "Mary Jane" shoes and she loved them so much, that when we put her to bed the first night, she wouldn't let us take her shoes off. She slept all that night with her shoes on. What a character she was.

In Sunday School, when we started to take the two kids with us, Kathy had to go to the bathroom. We were still working in the Spring Glen Sunday School and Billy Thompson helped keep care of the kids during the opening exercises. Kathy was potty trained at sixteen months and at that time would not for the life of her wet her pants. Well, Billy took Kathy out to go to the toilet but evidently didn't bother to take her in the portable potty. When Billy brought her in again, Kathy piped up in her little voice and said real loud, "Mama I peed on my shoe." Everyone in the church heard her and laughed.

Nancy was a very active baby and happy all the time. I would put her in her highchair and she would rock back and forth, making a lot of noise and eventually would fall through the tray space and out of the chair onto the floor. To be safe, I took her in the chair every place I went around outside and in the house. My problem was, the chair plus Nancy was almost more than I could carry. When I went outside to hang up clothes on a line strung between a couple of trees I had to take her too. Oh how she loved that. She laughed and screamed with delight. As the girls grew, our little house in the woods was growing smaller.

We decided to raise chickens for fresh eggs and Glen built a nice chicken coop. He put a high wire fence around the chicken yard and purchased some chicks from Washington Farmer in Renton. We thought they were all pullets, but they evidently had thrown in a few roosters to keep the pullets happy. Occasionally, we let Kathy feed the chickens and she would take her little coffee can with corn in it and go scatter the corn around their yard. Of course, I would go with her and the one remaining rooster that we didn't kill would take out after me to protect his hens. He never hurt Kathy but he was out to peck my heels. I learned to take a stout stick with me and one time in protecting myself I knocked him out cold. Wish I could say he learned his lesson, but he did not.

Kathy slept on the folding couch in the front room and we had the crib at the foot of our bed for Nancy. Nancy was real sick one time with pneumonia and I had to have a vaporizer in the bedroom with my umbrella over the crib to help keep the steam localized to help her breathe. All night long that vaporizer was hissing away. It was no wonder that Glen began to think we should get a bigger place. We had no privacy at all and the girls didn't have a quiet place to nap.

We decided to look for a house closer to Glen's work and near enough so it would be handy to attend our church in Renton. A builder had built a block of homes in an area called Lakeridge on Rainier Avenue just outside of the Seattle city limits. The houses were a short distance from Bryn Mawr and very near to Skyway Elementary School where the kids would attend when they were old enough.

These homes took up the entire block with sidewalks and landscaped yards. I would say there were about ten homes on each street. We chose and moved into a house, third from the top on 113th street. The houses all had brick in the front with large windows and an attached garage and they were very nice looking. Three bedrooms, front room, dining room, kitchen and bath seemed like a mansion in comparison to the house we had just left. The backyard was terraced with a nice space for the kids to play, beside an easy access to all the other yards on the block. I wouldn't venture a guess as to how many children lived in those houses, but we had a great neighborhood of young families. It seemed that sometimes all the kids in the block were at our place. Our place cost us $12,600 and how much we got for our little house in the woods I do not know. But a young couple bought it and we thanked God for the quick sale.

The Renton Boeing Airplane Company was down hill from our new home on the south end of Lake Washington and they were now building airplanes full time. We could hear the powerful engines of the planes being tested by running them hours on end without stopping. At first, all the noise of the motors running bothered us, but it wasn't long before we didn't even notice it any more.

Glen graduated from Northwest Bible Institute with honors and now was ready to respond to the call we felt to the mission field. However Glen was having difficulty with a swollen testicle. He went to the doctor and was told there should be no fear, as cancer did not have pain accompanying it. He was to go home and sit in a hot tub of water and take an aspirin. You know the universal remedy. The pain subsided and he felt much better.

Some time later he went to a University of Washington Husky basketball game with Rollin Michelsen and some friends from Calvary Temple and during the game he started to have that terrible pain again. He called me and I drove to the University of Washington Pavilion and brought him home. We gave him the tub and aspirin treatment again and the next morning I called the doctor and asked for the name of a specialist. Dr. Lombardini was insulted that we were not satisfied with his diagnosis but he did give me the name of a doctor anyway. I'm sure he thought as he had been successful with Kathy and Nancy he was up to Glen's challenge too.

We were able to make an appointment immediately with this specialist and Glen went to see what he would say. After the examination, he was sent home and before he reached home the doctor called me. The doctor said he was sure it was cancer but for me not to tell Glen. I was to pretend I knew nothing about the results of the doctor visit and let Glen tell me what the doctor had told him.

A date was set almost immediately for a biopsy and he went to the hospital thinking it was just that. The offending cancerous testicle was removed and no cancer was detected outside of the area. He was not told it was cancer until after the operation. He suffered for three months after, with burns on his back and intestinal cramps from the radium treatments he took. He was off work for several more months.

During that time, his friends at work bought Glen our first TV and installed a tall antenna on the top of our house in order to get a good signal. What wonderful friends he had. That TV helped him to be content at home while healing. We realized after talking with friends that no mission board would consider us for service since Glen had had recent cancer surgery. The direction of our lives changed again. What had the Lord in mind for us?

Glen was still going to SPC and working hard to complete his education. As I had sold my business, The Letter Shop, I wanted to do some part-time work in the evening. Doris Michelsen's sister, Velma Darst, had heard of a product called Empire Crafts Silver sold in the home from direct leads on a commission basis. It seemed to be profitable and she persuaded Doris to start selling it. After seeing the product, I felt it was something I could do now that Glen was home in the evening. It was serviceable and beautiful silver and most young girls would fall in love with it after seeing the presentation. One showing a night was all I had to do and if I sold a set I would make a nice commission. For practice I showed the silver to my mother and she bought it and then she started to sell it also. One week, I made commissions totaling $200.00. I stayed with the company for over a year driving all over the south end of Seattle to my contacts and making a nice piece of money for us.

I enjoyed decorating our new home and the first thing we did after moving in was cover our front room hardwood floors with a wool rug. Now days, they do just the opposite and take all those rugs up and display those beautiful hardwood floors. I made floor to ceiling lined drapes for the windows all along the front room and on the dining room window. I used a heavy dark green sea wave material with beige swirls. Being completely lined, it was a difficult job but when the curtains were finished, they were beautiful. We were getting our money's worth out of the Singer sewing machine we bought right after they started to make them again, after the war.

Our furniture was all second hand and very limited. But with two toddlers climbing all over them who cared? Phil made a rack to hang on the dining room wall to hold my collection of china cups. Glen mounted it there next to the door leading to the garage. Not long after it was mounted on the wall Glen came in from the garage and slammed the door and the rack with my collection fell on the floor. Thank goodness we had a rug on the floor that saved a lot of breakage. Of course, I lost several of the cherished cups that I could not replace, but it was bound to happen eventually as we had placed the rack in a poor place. Oh well, live and learn.

In the bedrooms I made ruffled valances with draw drapes to cover the windows. Rollin Michelsen had a preacher friend who made and sold knotty pine inexpensive bedroom sets and we bought one of the sets for our bedroom. I wanted Glen to put a bed light above the bed and I got in just in time to prevent him from putting a screw into the new bed's headboard to hang it on. He thought a bed lamp should be hung directly on the bed like the old fashioned clip-on lamps in their home in Bellevue. Being such a rough type headboard and so small in size it would have made little difference except we'd probably hit our heads on the lamp every time we turned over.

About that time, I discovered what I thought were worms in Nancy's panties. I called the doctor and he called in a prescription for a medication to be taken by the entire family. It was a purple pill that would stain anything it touched. Glen was reluctant to take them, but on the doctor's recommendation he did. Slowly, results showed up in the kids' diapers, which were stained a bright purple and an occasional pair of our underpants also had the stain. To keep the worms from re-occurring I also wiped all the kid's toys off with a disinfectant and in their books I wiped it page by page. After all of us had finished taking the complete series of pills I found out Nancy had eaten some cupcakes with coconut in the frosting and the coconut came out looking like worms. Much to do about nothing. I did find out what real live worms looked like later. Glen had made a sand box for the kids in the back yard and our neighbor kids also played in that sand box. We didn't know where they actually came from and in spite of precautions we had more than one household epidemic of the little rascals.

Hazel & Bill

Bill & his Banjo

Depression House

Margie & Shirley with dolls

Visiting friends in Fremont

Dance Recital

Girls with Dutchy

Glen, Ardis, Muriel at Homestead

Bobby with Bill

Shirley - Renton Cheer Queen

Scrimmage-Shirley, Bill, Phil, Glen, Presley, Pooch

Odle Home
4/10/08

Bellevue Homestead

Mt. Rainier Picnic before Glen leaves for Europe - Cross and Odle

Lt. Odle and Shirley at Neosho, MO

2nd Lt. Odle and Shirley at Empire State Bldg. NY

253rd Engineering Battalion – England

Frank and Inez Odle with Nancy and Kathy

Nancy, Cindy and Kathy at Lakeridge Home

Port Alberne, B.C.- Glen's Big Fish

Glen and Shirley's 25th Anniversary with Doris and Rollin

Dosewallips hike with Shirley's Mom and Dad

4th of July at Adam's Residence

Olympian's Council at Trostad's Cabin

50th - Glen and Shirley

50th Anniversary

Family with Glen on his 80th Birthday

60th Anniversary - Glen and Shirley with grandchildren

Glen with Mitzi watching Street Parade - 4th of July

Shirley and Kathy in Italy with Bob's Family

Jason, Ginger and Great Granddaughter Maddy

Chapter 16

Glen began to work the day shift as he had graduated from Northwest College and had dropped out of SPC just short of twenty hours necessary for graduating. He had been taking the Japanese language, thinking we might go to Japan as missionaries and had met some nice young people in his classes who were from Japan. Before leaving school, he invited a group of them to come to our place and make a Japanese dinner. Glen put up the ping-pong table in the middle of our front room and I decorated the table and put out my best dinnerware.

When they arrived, they greeted me by bowing in the traditional manner. They could hardly speak English and to carry on a conversation was impossible, but we tried to make them all feel welcome. One young man's first question to me was "Where is the toilet?" Glen told me later that the question was a polite one to ask in their culture.

The students carried box after box of fresh vegetables into our house and preparations began for the first and best Japanese dinner ever cooked in the Odle household. What a fun time I had watching them make a mess in my kitchen. Talking in rapid Japanese and happy to be making a traditional meal again, they just slung the food around all over the place. Smiles and nods were our way to acknowledge how welcome they were and how very much we appreciated the wonderful meal they cooked for us. After they left, I found some of the food on our kitchen ceiling. Honest.

In the summer of 1952 I discovered I was pregnant again. We really wanted to have a large family, but my difficulty in carrying a baby made such a dream impossible. But I was pregnant and happy in spite of the fact that the seven months ahead would be rough. Ardis, my sister-in-law, Margie, my sister and Glen's mother came occasionally to help me, as now we had the two girls who were three and four years old and I needed help. My doctor knew of better medications and I no longer had to have shots to prevent labor. I can't remember any real problems except the usual morning sickness that extended too long into my pregnancy.

My mother came over on February 6, 1953 to our house and cooked a nice chicken dinner for Glen, the girls and Grandpa Cross. I was in bed listening to all the talk, smelling the good food and not feeling too good when I had my first labor pain. I wonder if Cindy smelled that good food too and wanted to be part of the party.

Remembering my last two deliveries I thought that this would probably be a rapid delivery. Glen drove me to the Renton Hospital and before the next morning we had another beautiful little girl born on February 7, 1953. We named her Cynthia Inez. Her middle name was after Glen's dear mother Inez. She was the biggest baby we had had weighing four pounds two ounces. She had a perfect little round head with a lot of dark hair and we could see she'd be a beauty. How happy we were to have our three darling little girls, but daddy Glen had been hoping for a boy at every pregnancy. When he got the call from the hospital that Cindy had arrived he said "No, not another girl."

The girls were starting to bring home some of the childhood diseases and Kathy and Nancy had gotten the hard measles and scarlet fever when Cindy was first home from the hospital. The doctor wanted me to separate Cindy from the older girls. He thought I should take them to the hospital for a proper diagnosis and Harborview was the only hospital that would look at all three girls. We waited our turn in a room full of kids with various diseases and if they didn't have some terrible ailment when we got there we would before we left. When it was our turn the doctor told me the girls were very sick but he could not admit them. They had to have pneumonia too, along with their maladies to be admitted. He showed me how to give them shots and I took them home to care for a new baby plus two really sick girls. I was getting a nursing course there in my own little home.

I kept Cindy in her bedroom and the girls in theirs. Nancy was terribly sick and I feared for her life. When I went into Cindy's room I put on one of Glen's clean shirts over my dress and covered my face and head with a dishtowel. I wonder what Cindy thought when she saw me coming into her room with that getup on? Cindy didn't even get sick and we were so thankful for that. Both of the girls slowly recovered and after that ordeal was over, I landed in the hospital physically exhausted. Margie came over and took care of the girls until I was able to come home. Thank you, Marge, for helping me with my girls and both Ardis and Grandma Odle for helping me too.

We continued to go to Sunday School at the Spring Glen school house and both Glen and I taught classes there. After class, we attended the worship service in our church in Renton. Glen had a teenager's class and took them on trips and outings to keep their interest. I taught different classes and held the Vacation Bible School at the Village Chapel church in the summer. We sang in the choir and I was the secretary for the board in the Renton Assembly of God Church. Both the Sunday School and church grew and so did our family of faith. We were like one big family of close-knit brothers and sisters in the Lord and we developed a closeness that has lasted a lifetime. Looking back, I can't imagine how we did all that with two little girls and a baby too. What were we thinking going to two churches at once.

When Cindy was over a year, I decided to go to work again even though in my heart I felt God dealing with me to stay at home with my girls. In spite of knowing I was going against what I knew was right, I made application for work in June 1954 at Williams & Swanson car agency in Renton. The morning I was to start work, we were sitting at the breakfast table and Cindy was in her high chair. I had dished out her mush and set it on the table in front of the high chair tray to cool. She grabbed the hot mush before I could stop her and suffered a terrible burn on the palm of her hand. The skin came off her hand immediately and we rushed her to the clinic and the nurse dressed her wound. I didn't go to work that day, but I did the next. Would I ever learn my lesson?

I had made arrangements with Mrs. Page who lived behind us to take care of the girls. She was a lovely Christian lady and she was also a reliable person. I gave her my phone number at work so she could call me if necessary, but not all accidents happened when I was at work.

Cindy had an accident one time when I had taken Glen to the barbershop, before driving the kids with me to the grocery store. Cindy was in the front seat with me and we didn't have car seats or seat belts for safety in those days. We hadn't even heard of such things. She was standing in the front seat with her hand holding onto the back doorframe. I'd let the girls stand like this a thousand times, but this time I learned a lesson. After getting the groceries and putting them in the car I shut the door not realizing Cindy's little arm was in the door. She screamed and of course I opened it as fast as I could. It had split open the skin of her little arm just above the wrist and it started to bleed immediately. I didn't know if I had broken her arm or not, so poor Kathy had to hold the flesh together while I drove as fast as the law allowed to where Glen was having his hair cut and we made a fast trip together to the hospital emergency. Fortunately, it had not broken her little wrist but it was sure a painful "owy."

The kids were always hurting themselves and I should have been home with them to try to prevent some of these injuries. Here I had wanted a household full of kids and I couldn't stay home and take care of the ones I had.

Nancy's chin was constantly cut as she fell either on the ice or on something else. She would come down the hill in front of our house with her feet up on the handles of her tricycle, free-wheeling as fast as her tricycle would go. She went over the edge of the sidewalk and into the bushes more than once. With her recklessness, it's a wonder she didn't kill herself.

Our neighbors next door were a couple with one boy. Mr. Kolstad was the principal of Lakeridge Elementary School, the school Kathy and Nancy would attend. Mr. Kolstad was building a boat for their family and every Saturday and Sunday morning our sleep would be interrupted with him pounding on that boat. When he finally finished the boat they had the boat launched in Lake Washington and they used it for family outings on the weekends. One weekend during stormy weather their son fell overboard and Mr. Kolstad jumped into the water to rescue him. Sadly, both he and his son drowned. He never knew that all those Saturday and Sunday mornings he was building the boat it would be the cause of his death and take the life of his only son.

One day, when Cindy was little, I had dressed her up with a pretty little dress and her bonnet on and the girls wanted me to put her in their doll buggy. I did and told them they could take her on our flat concrete driveway only and play like she was their dolly. We had new neighbors next door and their little boy Kurt Priebe was a mischievous little rascal. He got some black oil and poured it all over Cindy in the buggy. The kids came screaming in the house and told me all about what Kurt had done. I felt like spanking him, but he got that from his own dad.

Dr. Priebe was a veterinarian in the area and besides the family, they had an Afghan hound with a long narrow head and long silky coat they called Seekre. When they let her out she bounced all over the yard and nearly scared our kids to death.

Meanwhile, where was Kathy all this time? She was suppose to watch them. Was she involved in accidents too? Well, she was the little mother who told me what the others were doing and was quick to report everything to me. She did however cut her eyebrow on the corner of the fireplace one time as she and daddy were roughhousing. But she was my little helper and always in charge of the girls' games and activities. For Nancy and Cindy it was like being in the service. They always had a sergeant looking over them.

I loved my work at the car dealers and I learned to operate the switchboard, greet people, and answered questions and typed up contracts. I got to see the original bill of ladings and what the dealer paid and then compared it with what the car was sold for. There was really quite a difference, which of course was their profit plus costs. Most of the salesmen were very nice, but one older man made me uncomfortable with his unsuccessful attempts to romance me. I got $1.00 an hour and worked there only eight months as I heard they were hiring at the Renton Boeing Plant for much more money. I figured if I was going to work I should work for the most money possible and the most possibility for advancement.

I was hired in the Power Plant Division of Boeing Engineer Department and worked for the engineers who were typing letters to various vendors and manufacturers of airplane parts. There was a pool of typists who either took dictation or more often, typed directly from what the engineer had written. For sure these guys hadn't had any penmanship lessons, as their writing was really hard to decipher. There was a head typist who would help the girls if they had questions on the letters. We typed an original, tissue, and ditto copy. If you made a mistake you had to correct the three different pages and at times a letter might be up to three pages long. The ditto page had a purple backing whose purpose was making multiple copies. Some of the girls were very skillful typists and could do a good job and others just made a mess. If you made a mistake it was not unusual to end up with purple fingers and faces. We had a soap that was used to remove the purple and one time in trying to get some purple off my face, I got the soap in my eye. I thought my eye would never stop burning. When we gave our letters for proof reading, if they were too messy we had to do it over and the head gal would give it back for retyping. Guess who didn't make many friends?

We had a beautiful blonde girl working in our typing pool. She was a strong believer in a different religion and would go to the restroom with her tracts and booklets and when girls came in she would engage them in conversation. She was also trying to get the job as the head typist. I had also put in for the job and was disappointed when she got it instead of me. But I didn't say anything and continued to do the best work I could. It wasn't long before the beautiful blonde was gone from our department and I had the job. I stayed in that department for two and a half, years and before I left I was Mr. Ed Rock's secretary. Mr. Rock was the head of the Power Plant Division and he was such a good friend of mine. He actually talked me into staying home with my girls and enjoying the short time I would have with them. That was very good advice.

One day, Mrs. Page called me to say Nancy was lost. I rushed home and after looking all over outside we found her asleep behind the Pages' front room couch. That was the beginning of my thinking deeply about leaving my job. I was making good money and getting $81.60 a week, the most I had ever made. In July 1957 I made a decision to put in my resignation to leave Boeing. Believe it or not Boeing did survive after I left my job.

Back home in the saddle I kept my home clean, my kids happy and my husband well fed. I settled arguments in the sand box, shooed the next-door neighbor boy out of my cosmetics in the bathroom and worked in my garden. Glen put a nice large rock wall on the west side of our property and worked up the border area so I could plant flowers. In the spring I had tulips, daffodils, pansies and a variety of annuals as the ground warmed up. Our backyard in Lakeridge had a huge fir tree on the edge of the property that the builder had fallen when building the house. Glen spent a lot of time cutting up the tree with the girls' help. We used some of the wood in our fireplace and the neighbors also enjoyed getting their share. Glen put up a swing set and our back yard was a gathering place for many of the kids on the block. I was now head of the park's department on our block. If I gave my kids a drink of juice I had to be sure I made enough for all the kids there.

Cindy's development was slow. She refused to talk and the doctor discovered that the tip of her tongue had a membrane that prevented her tongue from moving freely. We established a date for a small operation to clip this membrane and it turned out to be a simple procedure. She didn't even cry. After the doctor had finished, he stated there probably wasn't any feeling in that area. But she still refused to talk. Just pointed to the girls for what she wanted and they responded to her beck and call. I made an appointment with a speech doctor in the Green Lake District of Seattle for Saturday mornings and this doctor worked with her for some time and decided that she didn't talk because she didn't need to. The doctor said we should give her time and she would talk when she felt it was necessary. That was true, and when she did start we couldn't get her stopped.

In 1958 my dad retired from the telephone company. They had sold their big beautiful house on the ten acres South of Renton for only $22,000.00 and moved to Beacon Hill, in Seattle. Daddy had already bought his dream trailer and parked it in their backyard and was anxiously waiting the time when they would start out on their big adventure as snowbirds. The first year, they spent in Florida and enjoyed the warm weather and having access to fruits and vegetables of all kinds. Mother didn't like the bugs and the muggy weather was unpleasant so they decided to move their trailer to Tucson, Arizona. Some of their close friends had moved there already and there was a double wide available for sale in the court where most of their friends lived, and being in mint condition the folks were thrilled to buy it. Daddy fell in love with the court on Flowing Wells Avenue and they lived there until Daddy died in 1982. However, they spent all of their summers returning home and living on their new property on Hood Canal. When the weather started to change the first of September, he got the bug to head back to Arizona and he used the excuse that they had to get back to organize the shuffleboard teams. Playing shuffleboard was great sport for most of them in the park.

They had both men and women teams and there was great competition between the sexes. Then courts would play other courts' winning teams and they would end up with a trophy that meant for that year they were tops. Daddy's team was a really good one and they won many trophies. Fall meant he had to get back and defend this trophy. They had a great pool too and after a close game of shuffleboard it was not unusual for the losers to get dunked in it.

The clubhouse was also a big attraction for the members and on special days the women would cook a lovely dinner and if you ate you had to bring your plate and utensils and claim your spot at the table. Mother and Daddy had their 50th anniversary party there and the facilities were always available for the members' festivities, free of charge.

We continued to live in the Lakeridge area and we had only one car that Glen had to use to go to work. It was difficult for me to take the girls and go into downtown Seattle for whatever we had to do. I would walk with the three little girls down the hill to Rainier Avenue and take the bus. Cindy had her hair cut in Fredericks & Nelson's Beauty Parlor and she hated her short style. But the beautician said that cut would be best for her while she was young. I thought she looked darling but some people teased her calling her a boy. There was an attendant in the Renton

Standard Gas Station where we got our gas, who would tease her so much she would cry. He never did get the message to leave her alone.

All of the girls had narrow feet and had to wear special high top shoes for foot support. We went to a children's shoe shop in the Medical Dental Building for their shoes and they always got the same style shoe. When the girls got bigger I was able to take them to the Bon Marche for the style most of the kids were getting. It was a long time before Cindy could get her shoes there, but it didn't seem to bother her.

Nancy especially loved to ride the elevators in the Bon and pretended she was the elevator girl. She would ride in the elevator, punching the floor numbers for people who got on. She was still a little girl and I suppose people wondered where in the world was her mother. I kept an eye on her though and would stop her adventures when I felt it was enough. One day, Kathy fell down on the escalator and got her dress caught in one of the steps. It tore her dress and embarrassed her so.

When I shopped, I spent a big part of my time watching the kids as they hid around under the clothes racks or played hide and seek with each other. I'll bet the clerks hated it when they saw me coming to shop with the three girls. But I kept them dressed nicely and their hands were clean and noses wiped. When we left the Bon Marche it was still standing and we took home only what we had paid for.

In May of 1958, I went to work at the Washington State Department of Employment Security. Unemployed people would come each week and sign up for workman's compensation, and answer an inquirer if they had been looking for work and if they were "willing and ready for work." Mr. Cunningham, the Director needed someone who could take dictation, and I filled the bill. He was an impatient guy who, when he gave dictation, said only the pertinent facts and I had to fill in the blanks. I liked this type of work as in no time at all I knew what he was going to say and only really needed just the client's name. I saw so many people I knew there who were from school and who I thought were just taking advantage of the system.

I worked there until June of 1959 and in August 1959 we made another big change in the direction of our lives.

Chapter 17

*'The Lord is my Shepherd I shall not want. He maketh me
to lie down in green pastures, He leadeth beside the still
waters. He restoreth my Soul. He leadeth me in the paths of
righteousness for His name's sake."*

23 Psalms

I have quoted this psalm so many times in my life. Whenever I'm in a tight spot it comes to mind and I think of the promise of the Lord's nearness and His assurance of His help. We were about to step into the future with our little family in a totally different way and we definitely needed His help.

My sister and her husband Phil had long been looking for property over on the Hood Canal, just north of Poulsbo, and they called us excited with the news that the perfect spot had become available for them. There were also five lots about two blocks from the one they were looking at that were for sale. They wanted us to go over and look at these five lots and possibly buy them as an investment for our family. Phil wanted us to buy the first lot, Bob my brother to buy the second, the folks the third and Marge and Phil would buy the fourth. All of them were priced from $300.00 to $350.00 and at these prices they were a steal. Partial views of the canal made them much more valuable for future sale. A fifth lot that stood over a 65 foot deep well of pure water could be bought to supply enough water for the four lots. On our word, the folks and Bob bought their lots and we all shared the $500.00 cost of the well property. During drought conditions in the nearly 50 years we lived there we never were even low on water. It was a wonderful well and indeed a Godsend.

The lot on the water that Marge and Phil bought was 100 foot waterfront with a concrete bulkhead that faced north up the canal towards Mt. Baker. There was no way their view could be obstructed. After purchasing this land Phil built a rough little temporary cabin for the family to live in while he built their home.

The Youngquists and Odles weren't the only part of our family looking for either summer cabins or permanent housing to get away from the city. I think that Willard and Eleanor Odle were the first to purchase a cabin in the Grapeview area and the Odle family celebrated several summer occasions there together. Water ski boats were great fun and Glen loved having a chance to try his luck at water skiing. He hit the beach one time thinking he would make a fancy landing only to find out that the shore was immovable. He suffered the results of that landing for many days.

Then Middy and Marshall Adams rented Lillian Danielson's house at Harper the summer of 1958 to see if they wanted to settle in that area. Miss Danielson was Marshall's aunt who was a speech teacher at Seattle Pacific College. But the bank was too high for them and the house too far from the water to satisfy their family needs.

That fall Marshall purchased a place at Rocky Bay and worked on the residence so they could move into it the next summer. Right on the water with a nice beach, they used it as their summer place for 25 years. Marshall ingeniously built a floating dock attached to four pilings that would let the dock rise and fall with the tide. It was a wonderful place and all the family and many friends were invited to celebrate July 4th and other happy occasions with the Adams' many of those years. We'd all bring steaks or whatever our family wanted to barbecue plus side dishes to share with the families and the tables were always piled high with delicious food. Middy even made fresh rolls for breakfast and prepared large bowls of fresh strawberries and raspberries. No one went home hungry. The weather was usually nice enough to barbecue our steaks and eat outside on the picnic tables but occasionally it was a terrible 4th with rain and wind typical of Washington State. Thankfully, the house was large enough so they could accommodate a large group in the house and Middy had enough games to play to keep us all busy. When the weather was good, playing in the water, volleyball, baseball, horseshoes and lighting off firecrackers in the evening was usually the plan of the day. Whatever the weather, before we got home, the kids were sound asleep in the backseat and Glen had to carry them into their beds.

Marshall and Middy purchased another home in Driftwood Cove on Henderson Bay and remodeled it in 1983. They lived in it during the summer while still living in their Tacoma home during the winter. They moved full time to the Cove in 1989 and our annual 4th of July celebrations were held there until the present time. I wonder just how many wonderful events the Adams' family have hosted at that beautiful place? We celebrated the 60th 4th of July the summer of 2011. Romances developed, marriages performed, children born, new friends made and older siblings have left us one by one over the years. How long Middy will be able to host this annual event since Marshall has passed away only the Lord knows. But Marshall and Middy have been the means of our family celebrating together for all those years and we thank them for their generous hospitality.

The property we bought on Beach Drive was covered in the back with scrub bushes; scotch broom, wild blackberry, creeping vines and fir trees. The place where our house was built was relatively clear but it would take considerable work for Glen to clear the area back of the house where he would plant our garden. Marge and Phil invited us to come and share their cabin on the weekends and we did for a short time. We had purchased a sixteen foot travel trailer and had taken a couple of nice trips with it but mostly, it sat in the driveway of our home in Lakeridge waiting for action. The summer after purchasing our lot we took the trailer and put it on the property the folks bought because it had access to a dirt road that ran in front of the place.

Glen commuted to work at the telephone company taking the ferry at Winslow on Bainbridge Island and on arrival in Seattle he walked the short distance of one block to the Exchange Building where his office was. He and Phil commuted together leaving early in the morning and arrived home about six o'clock in the evening. With the long hours of sunlight during the summer it gave the fellows a nice evening to enjoy by the water. Our little family had a great time with the Youngquists' and we all especially enjoyed that first summer. However, when evening came it was really a trial, especially for me. The kids brought a lot of the outside dirt into the small trailer with them and I had to wash their feet and clean them up in a limited space before putting them to bed. The table in the kitchen had to be taken down and made into the bed for the big girls. The bunk above our bed in the back of the trailer was where Cindy slept. Then in the morning, when Glen got up early, we put the girls in our bed, and then made their bed back into the kitchen table. I cooked Glen's breakfast and when he left for work I climbed into bed with the girls. That routine was repeated every day except on the weekend that summer and I got so I was an expert in taking down and setting up the beds.

Living so near the beach, the men thought up every game they could that required all of us getting in that ice-cold canal water. Phil had a little rowboat and he put a buoy out in the water as a point to row the boat to and around back to the beach. The one who could do this stunt in the shortest time was the winner. Neighbors up and down the beach could hear us scream and yell when we either won or fell in the water during the excitement of the game. Sometimes, Phil also put a small one horsepower outboard motor on the dingy and the game was made more difficult as we had to hop in, start the motor, and make the loop around the buoy and back to shore.

Around the 4th of July, we looked forward to the wild blackberries that grew in the logged places in our area. If we found a patch that had really big berries in abundance, we didn't tell anyone where it was. We kept going back and picking all the berries until we had them all picked. One time I was instructing the kids to be especially careful not to dump their berries as we climbed over a pile of logs and would you know it, I spilled my own berries. Boy did the kids get a laugh. The berries we picked were not the big berries that grow along the roads in August and September, but the small ones that grow low on the ground in areas that get a lot of sun. They are the best tasting berries without a lot of seeds and they make delicious pies.

Glen put in some Marionberry starts Phil gave him from a farm near Puyallup that had perfected them. They were a combination of several berries and were absolutely the best berries for pies. I picked our berries and froze them for pies during the winter. Every year I baked three pies and took them to the 4th of July celebration. Willard made homemade vanilla ice cream to go on top and we had the best of all desserts.

We shared many meals together with the Youngquists. If Phil and Glen had dug clams, Marge would make clams on the half shell. She had that special recipe down pat and it was delicious. After cleaning the live clams, open them with a sharp knife and wash any sand from the inside. In a frying pan add the oil and get it piping hot. Place the half of the shell with the clam in a dish with beaten eggs and then into biscuit mix and onto the hot frying pan. Fry quickly until done. It doesn't have to be long.

Sometimes, we made clam chowder and I think it was one of our favorite soups. We used two different clams for our chowder. The native bivalve mollusks found in the sand at low tide or the gooey duck that you really had to dig fast down in the sand to get. Both make great soup, but the gooey duck clams are sweeter. To make gooey duck soup you skin the neck and grind it, setting it aside. In a kettle sauté onions, celery and cubed peeled potatoes in a little oil until they are done and add the ground clams with a can of evaporated milk that has been mixed with a little flour and water to thicken the soup. Add salt, pepper, paprika and any other herb, that you desire sparingly. Be careful with your seasoning amounts, you can always add more but you can't take it out. (If you buy live clams be sure they are still alive when you use them.) Serve piping hot with hard bread or rolls. Oh, that's so good. To tell if a clam is alive you cannot pull the live shells apart. If dead they will open easily and usually are filled with sand.

Nearly every night Phil would build a nice fire on the beach and we'd sit around telling stories, singing and roasting marshmallows. Oh, how we loved to sing those choruses. The kids loved the experience of the outdoors and after the summer was over we decided to put out a fleece to see if we should make the move from Seattle over to the beautiful Olympic Peninsula.

A small sign "House for Sale" was put in the corner of one of the front room windows in our Lakeridge home and we decided that if someone inquired and purchased the house then surely it was the Lord's desire for us to make our move. Every car that slowed to look, we wondered if this was our buyer. We had lived in this house only six years and had made some significant improvements to our place. Glen put in a backyard with lawn and flowerbeds, backed with a nice rock wall that divided the McKee's house from ours. Glen was always such a meticulous gardener and he kept the yard mowed and in first class shape. Low shrubs in the front of the house and in the brick planters made it very attractive.

It wasn't long after putting the sign in the window before a car stopped and a young couple with an older man came to our door. They were interested and wanted to take a look around. The older man was the father of one of the young people and he did a thorough job of looking both in the attic and in the crawl space under the house. The first time they looked, they told us they wanted to buy our house.

Glen had previously found out that we could sell the place with the buyer assuming the unpaid balance of our GI mortgage, plus the amount of the principal we had paid. A decision was quickly made that the price would be $14,400 for our home. I don't remember how much we actually got in cash from our little house in the woods but it was enough for us to help cover our down payment on the contract for our new house.

After selling our Lakeridge home, we rented a housing unit in Poulsbo behind the North Kitsap Senior High School. They were World War II houses built for workers at the Keyport Torpedo Station, and Bangor Submarine Base. The unit we rented was a two-story duplex behind the Senior High School facing the football field. On game nights, we could sit on the bed in the back bedroom, eat popcorn and watch the game. Phil Jr. was playing on the high school team at that time and we had an unobstructed front row seat to watch his team at no cost.

The folks were up from Tucson that summer and put their trailer on the slab they had poured on their property. My dad was so hospitable he invited just about everyone from the court where they lived and friends in their church as well to come visit them that summer. In August of 1959 when we made the move from Seattle, daddy and mother had two couples visiting them from Tucson. Glen rented a large truck and the men, plus Daddy and Glen completed our move to Poulsbo in one day. I stayed at our house in Seattle to see that the house was cleaned thoroughly and then I had to wait for Glen to bring the car back to pick me up. Not a chair was left in the place when the men left with the furniture and I had to sit outside on the flower planter and wait for Glen. By the time we got home that night to Poulsbo we were both really tired. But all our belongings were now on the Olympic Peninsula and we were residents of Kitsap County. Now that we were moved, what did the Lord have in mind for us in this little town of Poulsbo?

The house we rented had only the bare necessities. I didn't do any decorating at all and most of our things were in boxes or unassembled. Glen was commuting with Phil again to the ferry along with a couple of other passengers they picked up on the way. He liked the commute as he could get a cup of coffee on the ferry and read the morning paper on his way to work. The ferry was packed both in the morning and night and everyone knew which seat was his. If you were just an occasional passenger you had to choose your seat carefully.

Phil knew a builder in Bremerton, Bud Anderson, who owned Anderson Construction Co. and Bud gave us a bid of $16,814.72 for a two-story home on our lot. Only the top floor was to be completely finished. The basement was on ground level, and two by fours roughed in the rooms planned there. The bathroom, furnace, doors and windows in the basement were to be finished while the stairs to the upstairs were treads only. A deep sink by the washer and dryer at the bottom of the stairs was to be installed. No cabinets, closets or storage areas were even planned. It was really rough planning, but Glen felt the sooner we got in the house the better.

Glen got a loan from First Federal Savings and Loan in Bremerton for $12,200.00 and we had cash of $5,214.24. So Bud Anderson was hired to complete the home as contracted, minus a garage and stairs outside on the back of the house to a deck and sliding glass door to enter the living room. Glen planned to finish the basement, put on the garage himself and have the deck in the back put on by Tom Settle, an attendee of our church and a builder in our neighborhood.

I spent my days going to the property to help the builder wherever I was needed as a "go-for." When Bud got the top floor finished, I spent my days painting inside, as painting was also not included in the original contract. Glen spent his Saturdays painting the outside of the house as soon as the cedar siding was on. It was a big job for Glen, and he successfully completed painting that two-story 60 foot long by 24 foot wide house all alone.

One afternoon I had just gotten home to our rental in the Project with the girls from school and was starting to prepare dinner for Glen when the doorbell rang. When I answered the door a man was there collecting for a charity. He stated his mission and then he looked at me funny and said, "If you are having a hard time we will help you out. Just come to our facility." That's the first time I realized how I must have looked to him. A paint-spattered woman in a room with hardly any furniture in it and my hair tied up in a rag. I assured him we weren't in need but in the middle of building a house.

We had moved over in August of 1959 into the housing units in Poulsbo and then into the partially finished house in December of 1959. Glen had to shower and shave in the basement bath and I cooked on a table next to the deep sink. Cleaning up and washing the dishes in the deep sink was a real chore as there was no counter place. The kitchen and upstairs bath were the last things completed.

Phil had told us we wouldn't have to worry about power outages in the area, as they were rare. True to Murphy's Law the first week we were in the house Glen had to get ready for work in a dark basement by the light of a flashlight because we had lost our power.

During the football season, Glen tried to go to the North Kitsap home games and take the older girls with him. One particular night the weather was deteriorating rapidly, but being the sportsman that he was, Glen still took Kathy and Nancy to the game. He had built a nice fire in the front room fireplace for Cindy and me and we planned to enjoy ourselves at home rather than risk the possibility of heavy wind and rain. During the game, suddenly all of the lights went out and the field and all the homes in North Kitsap were thrown into complete blackness. There was confusion on and off the field and everyone realized this was a big storm and they had better get home as soon as possible.

Meanwhile out at the house we also lost our power, but the fire in the front room lit up the upstairs rooms and Cindy and I calmly kept our cool lying on the floor in front of the fireplace waiting for the lights to come on.

Glen found the girls and fought his way through the confused crowd to our car and home. He found us safe and sound in our cozy home awaiting their return. This was just a harbinger of the many future power blackouts to come that winter.

Chapter 18

The first Sunday we had moved into the housing unit in Poulsbo we drove a couple of blocks to Main Street to attend church in the Full Gospel Tabernacle. The congregation consisted of about 40 or 50 people plus children and it didn't take long to discover the people were mostly of Norwegian descent. Al and Erika Munger from Turlock, California had recently been appointed pastors of the church. Al, a tall lean young man with a wonderful sense of humor and his wife Erika, who was a happy friendly person and gifted musically. They had two girls, Trudy and Karen. Erika led the choir and orchestra and she also played a xylophone. We were warmly welcomed and immediately put to work in the church. Glen replaced Marvin Nicholson as Treasurer of the church and I took over as Sunday School Superintendent. Most of the people were either related or had known each other for many years. It didn't take us long to realize this was going to be our next church home.

The church had been recently redecorated with new pews purchased from a remodeled theatre in the center of town. In back of the platform was an apartment where previous pastors and their families had lived. Al and Erika however, lived in a home more suitable for their family in the town's residential district.

Our girls made friends immediately with some young people and we were pleased with the direction the Lord had led us. The women of the church had an active Missionary Society that met in the homes of members for luncheons and to work on sewing projects. We also packed good used clothes in containers to send to foreign missionaries and made quilts to take to the Headquarters of the Assembly of God in Kirkland, Washington. Occasionally, we would visit the Kirkland facility to see a large room that was filled to capacity with good useful items provided for missionaries at home or temporarily on leave.

Glen and I also sang in Erika's sanctuary choir and Glen started to sing in a quartet with Phil Youngquist, Rod Trostad, and Al Munger. A close bond was formed with this quartet and only Pastor Al is still living today.

Our home was finally finished as far as the builder had contracted and we loved it. Looking out my kitchen window I could see the wide expanse of blue water with Mt. Baker in the background. One task led to another and I proceeded to decorate each room until I felt the pressure intensify and what had been a joy became a burden.

As time passed I became more depressed and lonely, having left my church friends and neighbors in Renton. With the increase of more and more duties in my new home I started to neglect my time of reading the Bible and praying. Alone during the day and feeling blue, I looked out my bedroom window to see if I knew someone who passed on the one lane dirt road in front of our house. Why didn't our mailman come or the man who delivered our milk come up on the porch and talk a little while? Few cars or trucks ventured up Beach Drive and I started to spend too much time in bed.

One of the ladies from church, Thelma Nicholson, came to visit me and brought a nice casserole for our dinner. What a lovely thing for her to do and I appreciated it so much. Her visit gave me the incentive to face the world again. Little by little, I made friends with the ladies at church and joined in the activities provided there. I also started to get acquainted with my neighbors and they helped me regain my hope that this was our home and we had made the right move.

Directly across the street from us lived the Bill and Jean Chesney family. Bill worked at Keyport in the Employment Department and Phil knew Bill's family in Bellingham where they both had their roots. Jean was a Methodist minister's daughter and we became good friends. They shared their driveway with a single woman Emugene Mattson. She owned a large piece of land with a small cabin on the water that she wanted to sell. However, our piece of property, where the pump house was located, was directly along the front of her property line and prevented access to the piece she wanted to sell. With our permission she had our well property surveyed and we made up a Quit Claim Deed to reconfigure our pump property to be along the South boundary line versus the East line. She easily sold that property after the pump house lot location was changed.

Buster and Doris Paulson lived on the same side of the road as our home at the corner where Brownlee Road and Beach Drive met. Doris had her dad living with them at that time and Glen bought her dad's Plymouth car for an extra car for the girls to drive when they were old enough. Doris and Buster had one daughter Martha, and Doris still lives there alone, some 60 years later. East of us lived an older couple, the Scofield's. They had a lovely home and large fenced-in backyard with a nice big doghouse for their dogs.

The big waterfront Mattson home next to the Chesney's eventually sold to Jerry and Barbara Reitan. There was always some activity across the street as they had two boys and three girls who attracted many friends. Someone planted fir trees in front of the Reitan's and the Chesney's already had poplar trees growing in front of their place. It didn't take long for most of our view to be blocked. However, as soon as the Chesney home sold to Ron and Marcia Mack they cut down those poplar trees. Then the Reitan's also decided to cut their fir trees and we had our view back. I remember I sent the Reitan's a thank-you note with a small check to have a celebration dinner on us as their actions had opened up again the wonderful view we had previously enjoyed.

One night when Glen came home from work, he carried a mysterious box. The girls gathered eagerly around as he put the gift down on the floor and opened it. Timidly, in one corner two little eyes pleaded with Glen for mercy as he lifted up the cutest little toy terrier pup you ever saw. She was so afraid she couldn't even stand upright on the slippery kitchen floor. Glen's lunchtime walk usually passed a pet store on First Avenue in Seattle and when he saw her, knew immediately we would all love her. What a wonderful surprise for the girls. The girls named her

Tinker Belle and her name fit her perfectly as she wiggled right into our hearts and became a permanent fixture on the floor beneath our feet.

Sammy our Siamese cat had been injured in an accident before we moved into the new house and never was the same again. I had been packing up our things from the trailer to go home after our weekly visit and I stepped down where the cat was sleeping. I didn't see him and crushed his head. We took him to the vet, but there was nothing that could be done for him and he walked off balance from then on. One day he went out the back door and never came back. We thought he just went away and died.

Glen cleared all the blackberry vines and scrub bushes out of our back yard and proceeded to put in a lawn and small garden space. He bought a roto-tiller to help cultivate the soil and got a man to bring in topsoil for around the front of the house. Glen worked so hard trying to make our place lovely. The moles, weeds and scotch broom were a constant enemy and he seemed to always have a battle on his hands. Little by little our yard took shape and Glen's vegetable garden rivaled the one his dad had maintained.

Glen's next project was to select seven small fruit trees that he planted behind his vegetable garden and in a few years we had a beautiful orchard that was lovely all year round. The young trees supplied us and all of our friends with an abundance of fresh fruit and in the fall we had fun taking the apples to Johnny's Mill cider press. One year we made 40 gallons of cider to share with our friends by squeezing the fruit of just one tree.

Years ago, right after Kathy was born, we purchased a pressure cooker and food drier to preserve fruits and vegetables that Glen planned to grow. It probably saved us hundreds of dollars every year by his hard work.

Just about every year during the fall season I could run out in the garden and pick some corn, beans or other produce and we'd have it for supper fresh off the stalk. Oh so delicious. Love of gardening was passed down to Glen from his father who always maintained a wonderful garden and generously gave to others. Before we had a garden, Glen's dad would give us a sack of corn to preserve. He'd ask me how many

I needed and if I said twelve dozen, when they arrived there would be exactly that number. I could count on him always giving me no more or no less. Glen and his sister Middy were the only ones of his family that I believe received the desire to till the ground as his father had done. Middy still has a lovely yard with shrubs, roses, flowers of every kind and some vegetables in season. Her yard is kept in top condition and on the 4th of July, at the family gathering, it is truly a show place.

Glen started to complete some of the things indoors that were unfinished by the contractor and the bedrooms in the basement were first. The girls had been sleeping in their rooms without walls and they told us they felt so afraid in that big dark basement. I know just how they felt as we had the same unfinished rooms when we were kids. He finished their closets with good smelling cedar boards to keep the moths out of their clothes and in their rooms we hung wallpaper that the girls picked out.

In the basement next to the central furnace system, Glen built a large room with shelves and space for storage of my canning. I loved this room and filled the shelves with hundreds of jars of fruit, jams and jellies, beans, tomatoes, pickles, and corn. In the fall when Glen dug the dahlia tubers and brought them in to separate and dry, he put papers on the floor to keep them from molding and then boxed them in preparation for Spring plantings. Glen also wrapped the green tomatoes in newspaper and put them in grape boxes to ripen. We had ripe tomatoes generally right up into the New Year. He really loved to garden and in the summer during the growing season he would change into his farmers clothes so he would be ready to work outside after supper. When the girls were little they could always have a ride in daddy's wheel barrel along with a dog or cat.

His next project was to build the attached garage with the help of his father. Frank and Ruby, Frank's second wife after Glen's mother passed away, came and stayed with us until most of the garage was finished. You may be sure the garage was built to precise figures, as everything Frank did was mathematically perfect. We had Leonard Olson finish the garage completely by putting the wide cedar shiplap on the garage's exterior that matched the house. Leonard who was a finish carpenter did a wonderful job with very little waste of material. Then Glen had the garage door installed along with automatic garage door openers so we could drive into the garage without braving the elements. Another job was finished and scratched off the "to do" list.

Tom Settle built the decks on the front and back of the house with a sliding glass door installed at the south end of the front room. The back deck was a big improvement for us as we were now able to exit our front room onto the deck and down to the back yard. We put a table with an umbrella on the deck to shade the area and ate many of our meals there. One time when we had a large crowd Tinker Belle fell off the deck down into some bushes without even being hurt. She just picked herself up and came up the back steps and said, "Now where were we?" She had another fall down the stairs to the front deck onto the concrete below and spent several days in her bed.

One night, my father Bill Cross brought us home another little white kitty tucked under his coat lapel. We named her Saude. She had bright blue eyes and the tips of her ears were orange. Now we had another little kitten to love and play with. However, when she was fully-grown she was bitten on the leg by a male cat and the vet told us a male cat's bite was as deadly as a snake's bite. She just went away and died too. We weren't having much luck with our cats were we? The next cat we got was Barney, a black and white tuxedo shorthair that Nancy gave us. When we went on vacation I asked Marge to feed him and watch him for us. One night when Marge came up to feed him, Barney ran out to greet her and ran under the wheels of her car. That was the last of our cats.

I sewed many things for the girls and they were always dressed so pretty. Every special holiday they each had a new little dress. On one special occasion I had decided to make dresses for the girls using the same pattern but different colors and as usual I got a light aqua color for Nancy, pink for Kathy and probably blue for Cindy. Nancy was really upset with her color and decided to leave home. I didn't think she'd actually run away, but at dinnertime she was nowhere to be found. We all started to look for her and Glen found her next door in Scofield's doghouse. Other times when she got upset Nancy would hide in our small trailer that Glen parked in front of our garage. The only way I could get her out of the locked door was to offer her a candy bar and that would do the trick. She had a sweet tooth the same as so many in our family.

Glen put a nice six foot tall fence around the lawn in our back yard with a couple of gates so we could get back to the vegetable garden and fruit trees. We thought the kids would like an above the ground pool so we went to a pool supply store in Seattle and bought a large one. Our pool had a ladder to climb up and over into the pool and Glen installed a filter pump system to clean the water. It was heated by the sun only and at times could be really cold. To jump in the pool was a shock but it probably was the best way to get in. The Scofield's had some tall poplar trees just inside their yard and little bugs would attach themselves to leaves and fall in the pool. Glen had to take all the leaves and bugs out each night and then he would have his swim before he worked in his garden. Our girls loved the pool and Glen's time was well spent.

The pool attracted the neighbor kids and they would come to the house and ask to use it. If I was going to be in the backyard I would let them swim, but for them to swim without supervision, I had to say no. I guess everyone with a pool has the same problems.

It was so much fun to have our friends visit with their kids and after Rollin retired from teaching in Seattle they bought a home in Poulsbo and were regular visitors at our place during the summer. Doris would call and ask our plans for dinner and we would share our food and the kids would enjoy the pool while we played cards. Rollin and Doris loved to play Rook with the women playing the men. We got to know our partners so well we just about knew what their next card would be. The guys accused us of cheating whenever we won a game. We really did try to rig a game one time but we couldn't pull it off. One summer the Michelsen's rented a trailer and took it up to Lake Crescent. They invited us to stay with them and we did. The first thing we did when we got there was get the Rook cards out and start to play. What great times we had with our dear friends. We were so close to them that Joe, Patty and Jeanie still call us auntie and uncle to this day.

Chapter 19

Meanwhile, Phil started to build their house down by the water in that lovely location. Phil drew up the plans and did most of the building on his own. It probably took him several years to complete his house but when he was done it had distinct elements that demonstrated his building skills. His father had been a boat builder in Bellingham and all of the boys in the family worked right along with their dad and learned the skill of building a wooden hull boat.

After Phil finished his house on the beach, he built a charter fishing boat right in their backyard. When the boat was finished he hired Herb to skipper and handle a charter business for him in Westport. We were invited to go with several other couples along with Marge and Phil on the MissMinMar's maiden voyage to Westport. We got as far as Port Angeles and the boat hit a submerged log and tore a hole in the hull. The women all had to get off and go home, as the remaining trip was too dangerous for them. The men continued on their trip using a bilge pump to keep as much water out of the hull as they could. They ran into more trouble though when they got out in the rough open ocean and the Coast Guard had to come to their rescue in a helicopter. The Coast Guard had a really tough time dropping a bigger bilge pump onto the deck of the crippled boat. They finally got over the bar in Westport and the boat was repaired. Phil's boat was used as a charter for many years sport fishing for salmon in Westport until he sold it to a fellow from Alaska for use as a charter boat there.

We enjoyed many fishing trips out of Westport and enjoyed eating both fresh and canned salmon. Sometime when I didn't know what to cook for supper I'd take a can of salmon and make a salmon loaf and put a cream sauce on the top. Even the kids loved it. Some of the fishermen on the charter boat caught large bass, which they considered scrap fish and discarded them. If they didn't want their catch we took it home and pan-fried it and it was delicious.

While I'm telling you about fishing I must not fail to tell you about several of our fall trips with the Youngquists to Port Alberne, Canada to fish for spawning salmon going up the river there. They were really big fish and were tough to catch because they were not feeding but just jumping and rolling in the water. Both couples rented small rowboats and the fellows rowed while the girls tended the lines. We trolled at a very slow speed and hoped a fish would see the lure and take it. Some days the guys would row us all over the sound and we wouldn't get a strike. But one day Marge caught two 50-pound fish and put a canvas tarp over them to surprise us when we came in from fishing.

I didn't catch a large salmon but I did get a really big ling cod. When I got him up in the boat he was so big I couldn't believe my eyes. Glen gave him to a Chinese fisherman on the dock because Glen wanted to bring home only salmon. I was disappointed because I loved good cod. Another time I had a big salmon on my hook and Glen was going to gently gaff it under the gills. When the salmon felt the gaff he smacked the water with his tail, broke my fishing pole and I lost the fish. The fish had hit my pole so hard it broke my wedding band on my ring finger. That year we brought so much fish home in boxes on the top of our car that the dent in the roof never did go back to it's original shape. All the way home the car dripped with that fish smell and it took a good wash to get it off. Phewwww.

Margie was a member of the North Kitsap Garden Club and took me with her to one of their meetings. This was a large active club and each month they had a guest speaker to demonstrate some special flower arrangement and after the program we had a wonderful potluck luncheon. So many yummy dishes and the members came prepared to exchange their recipes. You'd think it was a cooking club instead of a garden club.

I joined at that first meeting, as I wanted to learn to make some of those beautiful flower arrangements. We had several holiday shows with all kinds of different holiday displays, some for sale and some just for exhibit. Many times we had a silver tea table with all kinds of cookies and goodies and our guests could enjoy the pastries and a cup of tea or coffee for just a small "silver donation." The money that was donated was used to send our club president to convention each year.

Some of the members would make craft articles or have plant items for sale too. The clubhouse was always decorated so beautifully and it was really worth a small entrance fee to attend and get ideas for decorating your own home. I was on the Christmas decorating committee one year and Glen was helping me get tables from our church to display the many Christmas items. He had borrowed a flat bed truck and was in the process of delivering the tables to the clubhouse side door. I was standing at the bottom of the stairs directing Glen as he backed down to the stairs to unload the tables. The brake on the truck slipped and the end of the flat bed came within inches of pining me to the railing. I thanked God for that deliverance. An inch or so further and I would have suffered a terrible accident.

Our club held a District Flower Show one fall and members were asked to make arrangements to fit a category of their choice. Being fall I had decided to make an arrangement out of colorful vine maple leaves. I gathered some bright orange and yellow leaves on long branches and got some large buckhorn blossoms and put them in a small container at the base of the leaves and placed the container on a piece of extra slate that was left over when they used it for our fireplace hearth. Everyone who viewed it thought it was a simple but beautiful arrangement. I didn't think it was so wonderful, but I loved the color of the leaves with the large buckhorn blossoms.

During the judging only the judges were allow in the hall and I remember waiting outside with the other contestants anxious to know if our club had won anything. My friend Bertha Hoovan, who was one of the judges, came out and found me and excitedly told me I had not only won a first in my category, but also the "Best in Show" award. What a thrill. That was one of the first times I had made an arrangement for a show and I wish I had taken a picture of it and saved the ribbons they gave me.

Bertha was a wonderful flower arranger. I learned so much watching her. Our church had her one time when we had a brunch during the Easter Season. She made at least ten different arrangements around the fellowship hall and when she was finished she explained briefly how the arrangements depicted scenes of the crucifixion or resurrection of Christ.

We had a large crowd of women and Myrtle Jordan was doing the cooking along with several other ladies in the kitchen. Myrtle was trying to cook the scrambled eggs all at one time using one of those large deep aluminum pans in the oven and she couldn't get it to cook through. All the other food was ready and the ladies waited and waited, drinking coffee and sampling the pastries. Myrtle finally resorted to making small batches of the scrambled eggs on top of the stove the way she should have done in the first place. The brunch took a really long time but the ladies weren't as worried about time as Myrtle was in the kitchen with her helpers.

A funny story also about Bertha comes to mind. She and her husband Ozzie lived out in the Foul Weather Bluff area and she would stop occasionally at our place on her way to Poulsbo. One time as she came up the steps on our front deck, a little chicken from across the street that had been picking around in our yard, spied Bertha and took out after her. For some strange reason it pecked Bertha's heel and made it bleed. I took Bertha inside our house and put a band aide on her foot to stop the bleeding. Now the night before Glen had picked a bucket of Italian prunes from one of our trees. The tree was simply loaded with fruit and I expected we'd have so many prunes I'd never be able to use them all. To try to placate Bertha I gave her the bucket of prunes. The next time Glen went out to pick the prune tree there was hardly a prune on it. The raccoons had gotten into the tree and stripped it clean. A trail of dropped prunes led from the tree across Bob's property into the folk's woods. Oh well I had plenty of prunes dried already.

The folks had their trailer on their property that summer and my brother Bob had driven over from Seattle to visit them. Our pastor Al and Erika came out to visit the folks too. The Munger's had a friend with them from Turlock where they had recently pastored and they wanted to introduce her to Bob. Bob was about 26 or 27 at the time and had never married. Ailene, a single schoolteacher, was the daughter of the Mayor of Turlock and was taking some courses at the University of Washington that summer. Every one was trying to match Bob and Ailene up. There were so many matchmakers in the crowd Bob didn't have a chance. When Bob went back to Seattle that night he asked Ailene if she wanted a ride back to Seattle in his little sport's car, and that's the beginning of their story.

Bob's acre was situated right next door to our property and because it had quite a bit of standing hay we let Leonard and Genevieve Olson have the hay for their cows. They raked the hay and bundled it up to dry before taking it home. After that year and seeing all the good hay in Bob's lot, Glen decided to buy a beef calf and raise it on our property. He got some barbed wire and fenced in the acre. He also put in an electric fence to be sure when he put in the beef it would stay in. In the front along the road he also put a wooden rail gate. We purchased a Holstein calf and named him Beefy Boy. That calf was so tame the kids had a great time playing with him. However as Beefy Boy grew he had no idea how big and strong he was getting. The Gordanier girls were playing one day in the pasture with our girls and Beefy Boy started to kick and jump around the girls just having fun. The smaller of the Gordanier girls was petrified. She just stood there crying and exciting the calf more. Then she fell to the ground in a ball and Beefy Boy put his head down on her and started to push. He didn't have horns so he couldn't hurt her that way. I was looking out of the upstairs bedroom window and ran as quickly as I could down the stairs and out into the pasture to pick the girl up and take her into our backyard. What a frightening experience for a little girl. Her mother was really upset with me and wouldn't let her girls play at our place again.

Our friends from the Spring Glen Church in Renton called and said they had a quarter horse that had one leg that would go lame if ridden too much. Chet Anglemyer said it would make a good horse for our girls if we didn't push him too hard. If we didn't take him for the girls to have as their horse they were planning to send him to the mink farm for food. Glen thought it would be a wonderful opportunity for the girls and when the Anglemyers' drove up with their truck there was Rowdy looking out over the cab with his ears up wondering where he was going. He was a gentle beautiful horse with a nice brown coat and white feet and undersides with a long white spot on his nose.

Chet gave us Rowdy's bridle and lead rope and Glen bought a nice saddle from someone who offered one for sale. I had to learn to put the bridle in the horse's mouth and the saddle on, and I was not too happy about that. Our older girls soon tired of the horse but Cindy was the one who loved and rode Rowdy most of the time. We got her a black cowgirl outfit, with a hat and a quirt to hit the horse with. The quirt was really more for looks than use, as Cindy would never have used it on her horse. When she got home from school at night I would put Rowdy's bridle in his mouth and put the saddle on him and I would lift Cindy up and on to the horse. She rode around the neighborhood and just had no fear when it came to riding that horse. To let you in on a little secret in all the time we had Rowdy I never rode him because I was afraid of him. He was sooooo big. Just to put the bridle in his big open mouth over his slobber dripping teeth was really scary. I did a lot of praying that when he threw his head up he wouldn't bite me.

Rowdy and Beefy Boy got along wonderfully. I think they were truly soul mates. They stayed together in the pasture and when Cindy took the horse out of the field the beef bawled until they came back. Beefy Boy was so smart he could lift the wood rails off of the front gate and at night when we were in bed we'd get a call from Mr. Ham down the block telling us our horse and cow were eating grass in their front yard. Then Glen would have to get out of bed, take a pan of oats with him and get those renegades back home again. Oh the patience of a long-suffering dad. The cow and horse would sometimes get out and get in Glen's vegetable garden and trample around eating the produce. Now that was certainly a different story.

Barbara Reitan came over one day and asked to ride the horse. Some kids were riding Rowdy and he was perfectly docile but when Barbara got on Rowdy that horse started bucking like a rodeo champ. I thought Barbara was going to get bucked off but she was able to hang on until Rowdy finally figured all that bucking was not paying off. Barbara's ride was really a short one.

Animals are not cheap to feed and of course we were feeding Beefy Boy for our own consumption eventually. When it came time to butcher him he was not an easy one to catch and put in the truck to take to Foss' Meatpacking House. But when we got him home again he was all cut up and wrapped in the appropriately marked packages. At first the girls were squeamish about eating the meat but they soon got over it. When I think of Rowdy and Beefy Boy I am sorry that we broke up a perfectly good friendship between a horse and a beef.

I don't know how long we had Rowdy. He was a good horse and normally without problems. However, one time after he had been ridden he was given some hay and developed a bellyache and he was really in pain. Glen called the vet and he said to get some castor oil and put it in a bottle and hold it up for him to suck on. We did what the vet said and he recovered in one explosive moment.

Another time Glen was riding Rowdy down in Surf Rest Park and dropped the lead rope and the horse stepped on it. Rowdy bolted and threw Glen and Rowdy came home without him. A little while later here came Glen all humped over and holding his shoulder.

During the winter we didn't have a barn to put Rowdy in so we got blankets and put them on him with big safety pins. There had been an old shed back in the trees that was almost all disintegrated and he stood in the cold out there behind what was left of the shed trying to stay warm. It was finally decided that we would have to sell him or send him to the mink factory. One of Cindy's girl friends wanted him and so we sold him to her. However we were so sorry later that we sold him because she literally rode him to death. His lame leg finally gave out and he fell and broke it. The Humane Society came and shot him to put him out of his misery. A terrible ending for so loyal a friend who obeyed Cindy's every command.

Well the friendship of my brother Bob and Ailene Christoffersen blossomed and we heard the good news that he had given Ailene a ring and the date had been set. This was a big event for the city of Turlock, California as Ailene was a well-known teacher and her father was still the mayor of the city. Their family's story is a very interesting one that demonstrates that if you work hard, use the talents that God has given you, it is possible to rise above your beginnings to anywhere you want to go. Enoch was a wiry determined outgoing young man with light reddish hair. He and his girl friend Marie were both of strong Scandinavian descent and when they married they had three daughters and one son. Settling in the area of Turlock he was not afraid to work hard and did so in rising from a farmer to one of the largest independent turkey processors in California.

Along the way he and Marie became affiliated with the Full Gospel Business Men's Organization and he was not only a generous supporter of their cause but an outspoken witness to the Spirit of God empowering men to live the Spirit-filled life. They had a large two story sprawling California style home with a beautiful large yard, nice swimming pool, rose garden and landscaping that would be the perfect place for Bob and Ailene's wedding. We were all invited to the big event and places in friends' homes were arranged for our family to stay. This was probably the most exciting event our girls had ever attended. They had new dresses and were outfitted to fit the occasion.

A room just off the kitchen that we would call a family room or rumpus room was set up with tables to display the many gifts given to the couple by their friends and guests. Mennonite women who were in charge of the food used a large tent in the backyard for food preparation and they did a wonderful job in preparing a lovely meal for the many guests at the reception. A German band dressed in red-striped vests and straw hats were hired to play the music for the occasion. What a wonderful wedding for such a handsome couple.

Bob and Ailene made their first home in Turlock with Bob working on one of the families turkey farms and Ailene still teaching school. After their first girl Kirsten was born they moved to Cheyenne, Wyoming where Bob continued his education to become a pharmacist. When Bob passed all his tests and was qualified to be a certified pharmacist they returned to California to begin his career.

Bob opened a drug store and pharmacy in Keys, California and my dad was so thrilled. He had always wanted Bob to be a doctor and this was probably the next best thing. Daddy worked with Bob and Ailene to stock their first store. The store had a relatively fair clientele in spite of the fact that it was in a poor neighborhood. I don't know how long he had this drug store but he was robbed a couple of times at night. However one day he was held on the floor with a gun to his temple while he explained where the drugs were stored that the robbers wanted. That's when he called it quits. For awhile he worked for other drug stores on a temporary basis but then he was able to find a wonderful job for the University of California at Stanislaus. He established a pharmacy in the Medical Department and worked there as their pharmacist until he retired.

Bob and Ailene had two daughters Kirsten and Tanya. Kirsten married Jack Alvord and they had three children Jack, Jared (wife Ashley) and Cheyenne. Tanya married Darren Porter and they had two children Jordan and Annamarie.

Chapter 20

"Another parable put he forth unto them, saying, The kingdom of heaven is like to a grain of mustard seed, which a man took, and sowed in his field. Which indeed is the least of all seeds. but when it is grown, it is the greatest among herbs, and becometh a tree, so that the birds of the air come and lodge in the branches thereof."

Matthew 13:31, 32.

In the book of Genesis where Moses described the creation, and how on the first day God divided light from darkness. On the second day He separated the firmament from the waters that covered the earth so that on the third day the earth could bring forth grass, herb yielding seed and fruit trees. The progression of growth resulted first, from light on prepared earth to sprout the seed that was planted. Even today that process has not changed.

We were at a time when God was directing us to grow and expand and experience the excitement of seeing His creative work. What new things would He sprout in our lives?. And what would be thinned out to make the garden of our lives more beautiful?

Before moving to Poulsbo in 1959, Glen and I had scarcely heard about the area and thought of it only as a bump in the road on the way from Seattle to Port Angeles to visit the Youngquists. I do remember that the North Kitsap High School basketball team played in the high school state tournament at the University of Washington and how seemingly impossible it was that such a small community could compete statewide for the basketball championship. When we started to come over on weekends to spend time with the Youngquists, Highway 305 skirted the Poulsbo's city limits and unless you turned down on Hostmark Street you'd miss the little city completely. There was a Chevron gas station on the corner of Hostmark and several commercial stores in the area but you had to turn down the hill before you saw the homes and small businesses that followed Front Street along the water. The First Lutheran Church, Martha & Mary Nursing Home, the Senior High School and the Elementary School were north on Front Street and the old Codfish & Oyster plant, and Standard Oil holding tanks were back on the south side of town. The Project where the wartime houses were situated was in the central area and south on Front Street in the middle of town was the little Full Gospel Tabernacle where we attended while our home was being built.

Our little church was crowded and inadequate and the congregation sought God's will for their future. Potential building sites were prayerfully considered and the property on Sixth and Harrison was chosen. Gordon Nickell, an architect from Seattle was commissioned to design the building. The people heartily approved his work and the first soil was broken in October, 1963. Glen was still the treasurer of the church and weekly he carefully counted the collections before I banked them. We were closely involved with the building of our new church and marveled that our small congregation was so faithful in giving, as God provided. When the congregation was able to see drawings and pictures of the proposed church, some marveled when they saw that an area was planned to install a pipe organ.

One of the questions so often asked was how can such a small church as ours expect to buy and install such an expensive pipe organ in our new church? The answer to that question was one man, Rod Trostad, who loved the Lord and was fascinated with the instrument. Rod Trostad searched the country for a suitable instrument and discovered a two-manual organ built by John Steere and Son for sale in Auburn, NY for just $1,200.00.

Rod and Glen took two weeks of their vacation and flew to New York to dismantle the organ in a Universalist Church. It had been damaged by a blast at the gas station across the street from the church. I can just imagine Rod's glee if he could tell you what a great time they had working together in packing more than six tons of organ parts which consisted of air chests, sixteen ranks of pipes (61 pipes per rank), panels, regulators and hundreds of parts that they dismantled to ship by rail to our new church in Poulsbo. What a lot of work those two fellows went through without the fancy equipment available today.

Rod and Glen were scheduled to sing in a quartet the Sunday before returning home, so they packed up their suitcases and took a bus to the town where Erika Munger's sister and husband pastored. When they got to Erika's sister's place, there was only one suitcase. Where was Rod's? Good thing that one of the fellows in the quartet wore the same size shoes and suit as Rod because it was Rod's clothes that had been left on the curb back in Auburn. Monday morning when they went back to Auburn the suitcase was still sitting on the curb where Rod had left it. Today the case would have drawn the bomb squad and all kinds of fancy equipment would have gingerly opened the case only to find a bunch of dirty clothes.

After arranging for the organ's shipment, the men returned in style, driving a brand new Ford Thunderbird from Detroit to a Seattle car dealer. Glen had always wanted that classy car for his own use and here he was driving home a dream come true. Too bad his back was killing him from all the heavy lifting and the fall Glen had through a hole they had cut to get the organ parts out. When they returned home, many dedicated and unskilled members under Rod's leadership gave untold hours of labor in assembling that beautiful organ.

For three years Pastor Munger and the people worked together to build a church that would be not only a place of worship and education for the community, but would also be a memorial to the Christ they loved and had followed through the years. On Sunday, May 15, 1966 a dedication of the beautiful little church was held and the scripture verse chosen was Psalm 118:23 "This is the Lord's doing; it is marvelous in our eyes." Those on the church board at that time were Leonard

Olson, Phil Youngquist, Glen Raygor, Glen Odle, Fred Watland and Kjell Schroder.

In June of 1966 a job became available for eight hours a week at Keyport Naval Torpedo Station in the Kitsap Credit Union office, and I was hired to cash paychecks and do other small accounting duties. I remained on this part time job for almost two years. Around the same time, our neighbor Bill Chesney helped Kathy get employment during the summer there at Keyport. This was the beginning of her working for the government. Now that she had some government work experience under her belt she could depend on getting future employment. That fall Kathy decided to enroll at Seattle Pacific College with a major in Psychology and a minor in English, as she wanted to be a high school counselor. Shortly after beginning college Kathy met a nice young fellow from eastern Washington, Dave Schilperoort, and they became sweethearts.

Nancy graduated from North Kitsap High School in 1968 and set her sights on a future as a schoolteacher. So many of Glen's family had been teachers and Nancy was suited with the imagination and happy disposition that would help children do their very best. Right after high school graduation she also chose Seattle Pacific College.

With two girls in college Glen needed some help with their tuition. I applied for work in March of 1968 and was employed in the office at Bangor Ammunition Depot during the loading of ships for the Southeast Asia Emergency. I stayed in that job only until I could get a better job in October of 1968 at the U.S. Naval Torpedo Station, working as a clerk in the enlisted men's mess for the Food Service Department. This job was really interesting, however a little lonely at times as I was the only civilian in the office with a warrant officer and naval chief. Hundreds of young Navy personnel ate in our dining room and there was always something interesting going on. When I got to work in the morning I could hardly wait to hear the crazy thing some young sailor did the night before. I was never disappointed as Chief Black amazed me with story after story that somehow topped the last one.

In 1968 when Nancy was a freshman in college she came home carrying a scrawny pup wrapped in a towel and we wondered why in the world was she bringing that dog home to us? We asked her who owned the dog and she informed us that we did. She had found him down by the canal near the college and he was hungry with no place to stay. She had been secretly keeping him in the dorm and felt she'd better bring him home instead of hiding him there. We already had Tinker Belle but our soft hearts could not turn that pup away. We named him Spock and he grew into a handsome mutt that we loved and Tinker Belle put up with until the day he died of a heart attack on the basement stairs.

On August 15, 1970, the year before she graduated from Seattle Pacific College, Kathy was married to her boyfriend Dave in Christ Memorial Church by Pastor Munger. Dave had graduated that year and would be teaching school. Kathy had a lovely wedding and she and I had worked together on each detail of the event. It was so much fun picking out the material for her wedding gown and the bridesmaids' dresses that we sewed with love for our beautiful and talented daughter's wedding. A loving God had given her to Glen and me and now we were intrusting Dave with her precious life. What would become of their union?. Would they have a family that we would be proud of? Only time would tell.

In the summer of 1971 I saw a job advertised in the Comptroller's Office at Keyport. It was a temporary job, as an employee had taken a temporary job in Australia and they were holding this job open for him, if he decided to return. It seemed that very few people wanted to take the chance of giving up their job and just getting nicely into the new job and then have him return. Because I wanted to get into the Comptroller's Office I decided to take that chance and was chosen as his temporary replacement. And true to my hunch a year or so later he came home and qualified for a much better position.

Cindy graduated from North Kitsap High School in 1972, and then finished a year's course at Bremerton Business College. About that time I was working in my new accounting job and a new college graduate came into our department who was on a disability grant. She lived in Renton and was commuting every day to work via the Seattle ferry. I asked Glen if he objected to me inviting her to live with us to save the long commute, and he said he would not. Her mother came over and met us and we were pleased to have Donna Herzog move in with us. She and Cindy became great friends and she was like a daughter to us.

Nancy graduated from Seattle Pacific College in 1972 with her teacher's degree, but permanent teaching positions were difficult to find. She found a temporary waitress job at the Sandpiper Restaurant in Silverdale and must have given her customers wonderful service because she received a record tip of ten cents. She was doing so well that the establishment wouldn't let her go until she got a teaching position in the Portland area. Finally a job opened up for her in Vancouver, Washington and Nancy started teaching, first part-time and then full-time in various schools in the area.

May 6, 1972 was our 30th anniversary and we decided to celebrate it with a trip to the Hawaiian Islands. Anxious that we look our best, I spent a lot of my free time in the evenings sewing clothes for us. I made Glen a couple of Hawaiian shirts and several beautiful muumuus for myself. We decided to go in October, as so many told us that the weather was perfect at that time.

On the recommendation of Bill Thompson we stayed a few days in The Breakers, a distinctive Hawaiian resort right on Waikiki Beach in Honolulu, and then flew to Kauai where our friends' son Joe Michelsen was stationed with the Naval Air Force. He showed us all over the island and then took us out to the beaches where they were riding the big waves.

Our final destination was a condo on Maui that was partially owned by Gordon Stenman, manager of the Poulsbo IGA Store. Our beach view was unobstructed and the lovely sunsets were mirrored in the clear blue water. That's where I had a real scare in the surf the first time Glen and I chanced the deep water. I saw this towering wave heading for us and when it hit I didn't know which way was up. Finally, when I got my bearings, I had been rolled topsy-turvy, over and over in my new bikini swimsuit that absolutely filled with sand. I thought I'd never make it to shore. From then on I limited my swimming to pools and shallow areas and crawled in the water with the little kids.

Wherever we went, there were singing groups entertaining visitors with island music and hula-hula girls showing off their costumes. Or was it their bodies?

One song we didn't forget was a song sung to Hawaiian instruments called "What Aloha Means." Just imagine in your mind that you are there, the trade winds are blowing your hair and the lovely hula girls in their grass skirts are swaying to the ukulele music.

"Aloha means farewell to you. Aloha means goodbye.
It means until we meet again, beneath a tropic sky.
Aloha means good morning, and always to be true.
But the best thing that Aloha means, Is I love you. "

What a perfect way to celebrate our 30th anniversary. Now I had seen how lovely the island was for myself in the arms of my sweetheart. Glen used to sing to me when we were younger and one of his favorite songs was "Let me call you sweetheart, I'm in love with you." He had such a pleasing voice and I loved to hear him sing. Even in church as I sat next to him, I would stop singing and listen to his mellow voice. One special song we sang together was, "The Indian Love Call," and when we got to the YOOOU's we'd drag it out. Oh, such good memories.

Back from our vacation we had to face the work that was waiting for both of us and replace the stars in our eyes with dollars signs. We didn't know that we had 34 more years to go and we would enjoy together many more trips not only in Hawaii but other lovely places in God's beautiful creation.

Kathy and Dave had moved to Yakima as Dave went to Central Washington University, working on a Master's Degree and Kathy went to work for Social Security. In 1975 they were expecting our first grandchild and two months before Kathy's due date we got a call in the middle of the night from Dave, telling us that Scott David had entered the world weighing 3 pounds 9 ounces. I couldn't believe it was Dave on the phone, as this was way too early for the baby to be born. Was having difficulty carrying a baby happening to Kathy just as it had happened to me? Gosh, I hoped not. The next day at work I didn't tell anyone because I was so afraid something would happen to Scott. Where was my faith? A few days later when we left for a little trip to Yakima to see baby Scott, I had to tell my boss and then it was out in the office that we had a grandson.

Dave was so proud of Scott and when we went into the nursery to see him Dave reached into the isolette and picked him up. His little head flopped over on the side. I was so afraid he had broken his neck. But God had brought Scott into the world and had a plan and a purpose for him. He grew into a happy little boy who rode his rocking horse with gusto, in the backyard at their home. Glen had always wanted a boy and Kathy and Dave couldn't have given him a more wonderful gift than a grandson.

I was doing well in the Accounting Department and new jobs opened up for me. Our Accounting Department was to be computerized and my boss Hal Crosswaite and I were going to a facility in California to see how the new system was managed. I knew nothing about the computer, but I was given a lot of info from the people there and somehow together we would be able to successfully make the change over.

Hal and I left for California on a Friday so we could go to Disneyland on the weekend before the next week's meetings. All day Saturday we had a fun time at Disneyland and my boss acted just like a little kid. When Sunday came I told my boss I was going to attend church at Melody Land Church, a large church near Disneyland. He was afraid for me to go alone, so he went to church with me. I don't know what he expected, but we had a wonderful service at the church and he seemed to enjoy it. He told me when we were going home, this was the first company trip he'd taken where he could relax and not be pressured to do something he didn't feel comfortable about doing. How important it is to live your life without compromise.

When we left our hotel rooms Sunday afternoon I thought I should go check his room to be sure he didn't leave anything. I was surprised when I looked and found a pair of white, women's pumps under his bed. I knew he didn't have a woman with him, but still I had a great time ribbing him about the sleeping beauty who left her shoes under his bed. When I left my job at Keyport, at my going away party, I had fun telling all his employees about the pair of white pumps under his bed when he left his room.

Around that same time, Nancy called and told us that she'd met a new friend and was bringing him home to meet us, but for us not to worry, he was just a friend and they were not at all serious. Well, when they came and she introduced Kevin to us, we fell head over heels in love with him. She might not have been serious but we sure were.

It wasn't long before Nancy and Kevin, against all odds, were married at the 6th and Harrison Christ Memorial Church on February 7, 1976 by Pastor Arnie Jergenson.

Our second daughter was now married and settled in their first home on NE 67th in the Fremont area of Portland. The next year they sold their first home and moved to NE 43rd in the Alameda area. She was teaching school and he was a Manufacturer's Representative for New Balance shoes in Washington and Oregon. Kevin was a hustler and everything he did seemed to prosper. Glen and I both started to wear New Balance shoes and haven't purchased another brand until lately. For a while Luann, his sister-in-law sent them to us free of charge. Thanks Luann.

When I got back from California with my boss I found out that our women's group at church planned a retreat and it was scheduled in a camp south of Port Orchard. I didn't sign up as it was on Friday and Saturday, and Friday after work was my day to have my hair fixed by Donene Munroe, my beautician of many years. I got a call from my sister Marge, asking if I could possibly take Friday off and go in the place of someone who had canceled. I told her I would go with her, only if she would wait to go until after I had my hair appointment on Friday. I haven't fixed my own hair for most of my life and to go to a retreat without having it done, I would be a mess.

I am so glad I went with her, as it was a wonderful retreat and our speaker spoke on using our gifts for the Lord. When she finished one session, she said she felt the Lord had a word for someone there. The room was in complete silence and no one responded. When we got back to our cabin, Irene Lanning said she was the one with the message from the Lord but didn't see how it fit the occasion. We asked her to tell us, and she said it wasn't much of a message but she would tell us anyway. "My child I love you, and if you will obey me I will give you the desires of your heart." Well the whole story is too long to explain but the word was for me. I had been putting off God's direction in my life for too long and I knew I should leave my job and obey him in a ministry He had for me. I told the girls there in our cabin the message was for me, but I was still struggled before I'd say yes to the Lord. Even then I had a stipulation.

I had a plan that when I got home and told Glen all about the retreat I would not tell him about the Lord's prompting for my obedience for service. Instead I'd wait for Glen to ask me to leave my job. If he did I would surely know God had something He wanted me to do. Well, I did tell Glen all about the retreat and the good time we had and when I finished he said. "Honey, I think you should quit your job." I was flabbergasted. Wow, in the natural Glen would never ask me to do such a drastic thing, as he knew how much I loved my job. This really was God speaking to me through my husband and it was time for me to obey my husband, as well as the Lord. How many years had I resisted the Lord's prompting and He was still waiting for me to respond.

The next Sunday, in the church bulletin, a job in the accounting department was advertised and I thought that must be it. Loving figures and accounting I had tried so hard to get into that department at Keyport and now was I to leave it for another accounting job in the church? But then I felt a check in my heart to wait.

A couple of Sundays later, I was walking from the church on 6th & Harrison over to the Poulsbo Elementary School and Pastor Munger stopped and asked me if I wanted a ride to the school where I taught my women's class. Pastor told me about a ministry he had been considering. Not a job in any department but a person to organize the women of our church and assist the Pastor wherever needed. While he was explaining his vision, the Spirit of God confirmed in my heart that this was what He had for me.

I told·Pastor Munger I would pray about it, talk to Glen and then let him know if I felt I could do it. I knew that I would do it, as I knew deep in my heart this was what He was calling me to do. The next week the deaconesses of the church came to my home and restated our Pastor's ideas. I gave the ladies the same answer I had given Pastor Munger. I had dragged my feet too long. I felt the Spirit urging me to make a public decision. "Shirley, it's time you followed the Lord."

Because Glen had suggested I leave my present job, on August 1977, I resigned from Keyport and started in an entirely new direction for the Lord. I felt my call for this full-time job. I was happy to respond to this ministry, to the Lord, and a salary was not necessary.

A telephone was connected in Room 18 in the old Poulsbo Elementary School and a desk and typewriter with a couple of chairs were put in the room and I was in business. We were ready to go someplace that only the Lord knew where we were going. Each lady who responded to His call were really blessed.

The first council of women who worked with me were all college educated and they were skilled in the areas where they volunteered to minister. It was because of their united efforts that we were able to present a program that was a wonderful testimony to God's leading of the women in our church.

During my time in this position, I was able to present what we had done to many interested churches and helped them also organize their own Women's Ministry. We had studies, luncheons, and retreats, brought ministry teams to our church, singers, films and church wide dinners. We started clothing exchanges for children, weight loss classes, exercise classes, Manna Ministries program (a food ministry for needy), holiday food baskets. We had fairs to teach our women to cut hair, bake. We made a cook book, had many Christmas bazaars and rummage sales. And on and on. We found out that busy women were happy women and anyone who wanted to minister could find a place to use her talents. What a wonderful group of women we had in our women's council and it wasn't what I was doing but the Lord.

Glen retired from the phone company after 37 years of service, on March 7, 1978. After his telephone retirement party, Glen and I went to Arizona to visit the folks. Kathy was experiencing some problems with her second pregnancy and we stopped to visit them on our trip south. Arrangements were made for Cindy to come and be with her until she was ready to deliver.

When we reached Tucson to be with the folks, we got a call that Jason Todd had entered the world early on March 18, 1978 weighing 5 pounds 12 ounces and was a strong little boy. Kathy and Dave now had their family and grandpa Glen had another grandson to love.

When we returned home to beautiful Kitsap Peninsula and Hood Canal, the area looked mighty good to us. How could anyone retire to Arizona when they had it so good here?

The ministry to the women in the church was increasingly interesting and I loved the opportunity the Lord had given me. Also, Glen was happy working around our home and he had two grandsons who were the delight of his life. What more could we want?

Now with the help of Jim Wise, Glen was able to completely revamp our front yard and make it a place of beauty. This major front yard revision was digging out nearly twenty years of trees and shrubs, relocating the driveway and fashioning a beautiful patio surrounded by Japanese cherry trees, mugo pines and rhododendrons. As usual, Glen did a wonderful job.

In June of 1978, the Kitsap County Herald published an article about the breaking of ground for our new church building on the elementary school property the church had purchased for $175,000 with the intention of expanding the church's facilities. The article read as follows:

"Members of Christ Memorial Church will officially break ground for their new church building Sunday. The new structure, which will be located just south of the former Poulsbo Elementary School between Lincoln and Hostmark streets, will be the fourth building to be occupied by the expanding congregation since it was formed in the 1920s.

The wood, stucco and stained glass building will seat nearly 1,000 for worship services. Other facilities will include a chapel seating 160, adult classrooms, nursery and day care center, an office complex and parking for 335-400 cars. A four-manual, 35-rank pipe organ is already at the site, ready for installation. The building was designed by the Seattle firm of Gabbert Associates working with the local building committee chaired by Don Green. Committee members include Conrad Green, Burrell Jull, Bob Lowe, Ruby Watland and Bruce Samuelson. Kruger Construction Company of Yakima will serve as the contractor."

"The ground breaking ceremony will begin during the regular worship hour at 10:15 a.m. The entire congregation will leave the temporary gym sanctuary of the old school and form an outline of the perimeter walls of the new building. Each family is invited to bring a shovel and participate in the symbolic beginning of construction. The church project is expected to be completed in 10 months to one year, and cost $1.5 million. "

What a thrill when the project was completed. My office was situated next to Business Administrator, Bruce Samuelson's lovely office and looked out on beautifully landscaped gardens and the school buildings. I saw the elementary children playing on their swings in their playground, so full of life and potential.

What a pleasant office the Lord had provided for me, so much better than any office I might have had at the Torpedo Station. Here in Christ Memorial Church we were about educating children, winning the hearts of men and women and helping them live their lives for Christ, rather than producing torpedoes for submarine combat.

The big news reported in the Bremerton Sun on Wednesday, February 14, 1979 was that "a Pacific storm on Tuesday, February 13, 1979 with winds of 100 mph in some stretches along the Washington coast wiped out the Hood Canal floating bridge. A trucker reported a harrowing four hours and fifteen minutes experience on the bridge wrestling his $36,000 three-axle tractor and semi-trailer against winds measured at 106 MPH. Unfortunately his rig was empty and every time he tried to back the empty truck off the bridge the wind would blow him against the bridge.

He resisted all efforts to get him to leave his rig and escape off the bridge with the bridge workers. When he finally reached the steel connecting section he looked back and toward the middle of the bridge and saw a piece of it disappear. He gave his truck all the power he had and shoved the rig straight back up the steel section that connected with the pontoons until he hit the blacktop. At the same time the twelve foot high waves snapped giant bolts like twigs, broke cables holding a dozen bridge pontoons together and the water tight compartments breached and were sent 340 feet to the bottom of Hood Canal."

The only person I know who was an eyewitness, was my sister Marge who was standing at her kitchen window watching the bridge when it went down. The bridge, built in 1961 at a cost of $26.7 million linking Kitsap County and Jefferson County, could no longer carry the over 5,000 commuters who crossed the bridge daily.

Their choices now were to drive the two hour trip around the canal or have the State build a temporary dock at Lofall and use ferries. The Jefferson County dock was still available for use on the west side of the canal. Sixth District Congressman Norm Dicks said it would take about two years to restore the bridge so to solve the problem the government made available emergency relief dollars to restore temporary ferry service between Lofall and Jefferson counties.

A temporary docking facility was installed in the Lofall area and also a local concession stand was built. Our daughter Cindy was hired to work with Adrianne Kinsey selling ice cream, coffee, sandwiches etc. to those waiting, sometimes over two hours to catch the ferry. At busy times, a line of cars extended out to Highway 3 and up the hill past Hilltop Tavern. Morning and evenings it was a major traffic jam. Think of this lasting for about two years. The traffic was not only coming from Poulsbo and points south but from Seattle and the Edmonds-Kingston ferry line north. The little community of Lofall was reminded daily of that big storm in 1979.

As our area grew, attendance in the church grew steadily month after month and services were adjusted to accommodate crowded conditions. An 8 a.m. service was added to the 9:30 a.m. and 11:00 o'clock morning schedule. Glen especially liked the early one, as we could attend church and then could get home in time for him to watch the football game on TV. I think a lot of other men and women liked this service too, as it left more of their Sunday to enjoy.

One Sunday morning, during greeting time, I welcomed a young sailor behind me to the service and after learning he was single and batching, I invited him to Sunday dinner. He was not able to come that Sunday and because his submarine was due to leave soon, I didn't see him again for nearly a year. At that time, Cindy had a couple of other fellows she was dating and to tell the truth my motive was not to be a matchmaker. I simply wanted to give a sailor a home cooked meal.

The next time I saw Bill, my father and mother were having dinner with us and I asked Bill to come along to join the crowd. My dad nearly talked his leg off and Cindy and Bill didn't even have an opportunity to get acquainted. However, it didn't take Bill long to ask her out and to make a long story short, she found a perfectly wonderful Christian guy that both Glen and I were delighted to add to the family.

Pastor Al Munger married Cindy and Bill August 29, 1981 in the new sanctuary at Christ Memorial Church. Donna Herzog who was still living with us and very close to Cindy, was her maid-of-honor and Kathy and Nancy were her bridesmaids. I made all the dresses except Cindy's, which was purchased from a bridal shop in Seattle. Silk flowers were arranged in small baskets for the girls to carry and Cindy had a lovely bridal bouquet.

My best friend Doris Michelsen and her daughter Patty Laschinski catered the wedding buffet. Ruth and George Edgley grew the flowers used for decorating the service, and Gail Stivers arranged them attractively on pedestals on the platform. Cindy looked so beautiful with her new handsome sailor husband. Now all three of our girls were married and gone and we were alone in our big home and for the first time, wishing for their voices to fill those empty rooms again.

The morning after Easter in April 1982, we received an early morning call that they had taken Grandpa Cross to the hospital with either a stroke or brain aneurysm. Mother said they had had a great Easter and after the morning service had eaten a lovely Easter dinner with the occupants of their mobile home park. Daddy savored several cups of coffee the doctor had previously told him he should not drink and that night evidently suffered his medical emergency.

On hearing the news, Margie and I packed hurriedly and the fellows drove us to SeaTac Airport. We took the first plane available and arrived in Tucson, too late to tell our dear father goodbye. The guys followed as soon as they could in Phil's car and arrived just in time for the funeral services.

So many people loved Daddy and the service was filled with relatives and friends from their Tucson church and mobile home park. After the service, his casket was placed on a cart and rolled out of the chapel to the burial plot with everyone silently following behind in a serpentine line. The grass was dry and lifeless in the cemetery and so was the ground around the tent that covered the plot where his casket would rest. After a brief ceremony, our goodbyes said, the workers lowered our father into the grave where his body would await "the trumpet sound, when the dead in Christ would rise and be caught up into heaven forever to be with our Lord." We were comforted with those words. We would see our daddy again some day.

Mother took Daddy's death so hard, but she felt she wanted to stay there in Arizona where they had lived for 24 years and where most of their friends lived. I went to the supermarket and purchased a large frozen turkey and cooked it. After we had enjoyed our turkey dinner, I sliced it up and put it in baggies to freeze so she would have plenty to eat when we left. I wonder how in the world she ate so much turkey. Bet she gave a lot of it away.

We helped with the necessary business following the death of a spouse, honoring all her requests, and then the four of us drove home. It was only approximately one year before mother sold her mobile home in Tucson, at a ridiculously low price and we brought her home to Silverdale to rent a lovely apartment, where she lived happily for seven years.

Cindy and Bill were still living in their Gamblewood home when their first baby Jennifer Marie was born in the Bremerton Naval Hospital on October 17, 1982. It was Sunday morning and at church, Paula Michelsen told us how to get up the back stairs to the nursery area before visiting hours to get a glimpse of our first granddaughter. On arrival in the nursery, there was Bill with a hospital gown and hat on, rocking Jennifer in a big rocking chair. He was so overcome with joy, he could hardly speak.

She was a beautiful little girl and wrapped up in that tiny body were all kinds of talents and abilities. When mother and baby came home, I helped Cindy out occasionally and Jennifer and I developed a close bond that is so precious to me.

Bill's submarine base was transferred to San Diego and they sold their home in Kingston and moved into a rental house in El Cajon,

California. That was a long way to go to see our kids. As Bill was on a fast-attack sub, Cindy never knew when he would be home or when he would be out to sea.

The neighborhood wasn't the best and Cindy felt really unsafe there. But Jennifer was happy and thrived in the lovely warm weather. They got a season entrance ticket to the San Diego Zoo and Jennifer called it her zoo. She loved to pet the animals and be pushed around in her stroller. We gave her a little lunch pail and she carried her treats around everywhere she went. Several years later Bill was transferred back to Bangor, to a Trident sub and they were able to settle permanently in the Kitsap area.

I was still Director of Women's Ministry in 1982 and had my head in the sand so much of the time. Being busy and involved with my many activities, I was not aware that Glen was lonesome during the day when I was gone. When I spoke at luncheons to women I jokingly said my husband was happy working around our place (and he was) and if I left him a jar of peanut butter for his lunch he was happy. Well, he wasn't.

Mother recognized this and told me how sorry she felt for him day in and day out, alone, while I was enjoying myself. As I thought deeply about our relationship, I realized I had fulfilled my job of organizing the church's women's ministry and the women were adequately accomplishing theirs. Now I should do my job as my husband's helpmate.

After I had my eyes opened, it was with great reluctance I gave Pastor Munger notice that I felt I should make a change. The following Sunday I made an announcement to the church I was leaving as Director of Women. It took me awhile to realize that being retired with Glen could be so much fun. We could golf every Monday at Rolling Hills Golf Course, take off when we wanted to see the girls, or go out to eat at some different restaurant, if I didn't want to do the cooking.

We started to work as a team and I found out that life wasn't over, in fact the most exciting period of our lives was just ahead. To be 60 and 62 doesn't mean we should be singing the song "Is that all there is?"

Chapter 21

In Psalm 90:12 it says "So teach us to number our days, that we may apply our hearts unto wisdom," or in other words count carefully the days God has given you and don't squander them carelessly or let the years slip away without accomplishing something worthwhile.

There were so many different ministries in the church, programs for toddlers, children, teens, singles, couples, women and so little for the founders and prayer warriors of the church. These people needed to be encouraged, have fellowship and feel they were loved. I had approached Pastor Munger in the 1970's with ideas for someone to organize a program for our seniors. It wasn't until 1982 that an opportunity now actually faced us to take over the reigns of such an organization and lead it.

We had a luncheon in the narthex of the church and presented the seniors with our ideas and asked them to respond with things they would like to do. The place was packed and it was amazing how excited they were with the prospect of a ministry for them. They began to rejoice in the fact that their time of service and usefulness was not a thing of the past, but in fact the most exciting period of their lives was just ahead.

At the same time, Nancy and Kevin had wanted to have a family and Nancy was having difficulties. All kinds of weird things happened to her and finally after having lost several babies, her doctor used a new technique and she was able to carry her baby to term. On delivery however, we nearly lost Nancy and it was only by the grace of God that different doctors were available to help her with the right blood, all ready there in the hospital for several transfusions. She ended up having a hysterectomy to save her life.

Meanwhile, a host of friends stood by in prayer for her in the hospital waiting room and chapel and all over the Northwest and California. When she came out of the delivery room we could hardly tell it was our Nancy. But in spite of all she suffered she was at last able to hold in her arms her darling little Meredith Kathleen born on February 11, 1983. I don't think I ever saw a more beautiful baby girl. Her long fingers were not like any in our family and I felt that she was destined to be a concert pianist for sure.

We stayed with the new parents for moral support and to help with Meredith after Nancy returned from the hospital. I was so skittish when I held that little porcelain sweetheart, I wasn't much help to Nancy. But I could cook and help Nancy regain her strength in other ways and I did.

When we went home, Glen and I continued to work on forming the senior ministry in the church. A group of active senior couples volunteered to make up our first seniors' council and they were the Youngquist's, Trostad's, Kennedy's, Samuelson's, Lampley's, and Ruth Borge. We met each month for a potluck and to finalize the plans for the coming month's activity.

A home office was set up in the bedroom Cindy had had just off the kitchen and we put in a desk, filing cabinet, couch, installed a new rug and painted the walls. This was the official Olympians' office right there in our home. I spent hours planning trips and surveying possibilities and then ran them by Glen. I had the wild ideas and he was the one who was level-headed and cautious.

My filing cabinet was filled with possible activities that I read about. Articles regarding new restaurants, parks, coming special celebrations, fairs or productions, special gardens and garden shows, unique towns etc. and they were placed in a section North, South, East or West in relation to where the church was and to Poulsbo. If we went north one month, the next month we'd go another direction. We tried to keep it interesting for our people just as I did in Women's Ministry.

Each year in January, I set up all the trips for the year and we met monthly with the council to finalize them. When we were in accord

I made reservations for motels, retreats, restaurants and contacted speakers well in advance of the monthly date. One of Glen's retirement perks from the telephone company was free long distance and local service so all the calling I did, didn't cost us a penny.

Glen and I tried to visit each place and scope it all out including coffee and potty stops. We tried to never go into a place where they didn't expect us. When we planned the Alaska Cruise we started with a cruise night on Nov 13th to prepare for the cruise the following June.

We always gave our members plenty of time to sign up and we also sent for tickets and reserved rooms in the hotels, all in plenty of time so things would work out well. Sometimes a planned trip had to be changed, but we weren't discouraged as we found this ministry to seniors was the Lord's and He closes and opens doors as He wills. A closed door almost always means He has a better event planned for us. There are unlimited places of beauty and interest in our great state and with advanced planning our seniors could have a program that would not only delight them, but also provide an opportunity for them to invite their unchurched friends exposing them to the joys of Christian fellowship.

We had our first Sunday School Class in the Fireside Room on January 11, 1987 with Ed Parr as our teacher and Marge Youngquist as our pianist. It wasn't long before this room was so packed that you had to come early to find a seat. We had coffee and delicious treats each week provided by our women. I can't remember all the wonderful teachers we had but God always supplied us with just the right person to bless our members.

During the ten years Glen and I were the Olympians' leaders we had 120 monthly trips with only one event being canceled because it was the day of the funeral of one of our members. We had eight retreats, three at Warm Beach Senior Center, three at Cannon Beach Oregon, and two at Falls Creek.

We had a fall and spring retreat at Harrison Hot Springs in Canada, spent time in Victoria and toured Buchart Gardens and had high tea in the Empress Hotel. At the Empress Hotel they had so much food prepared they packaged it up and we took it with us to eat later when we had our game time. What a terrible night I had after eating all that rich food. I didn't know they weren't expecting me to eat it all myself. Good thing I had my Mylanta with me or I would have been sick the next day.

We had so many places we visited and great experiences that were fun in the ten years we enjoyed working with the Olympians that it would take a complete book to tell about all of them. Each month I wrote a letter to all the Olympians reviewing our current adventure in order that those who could not travel with us could at least vicariously enjoy the fun. At that time I could conservatively say we had over 100 people on our mailing list. The big yellow bus carried about 46 people and many times we had not only the bus, but two vans full of people.

In 1992 we felt we were getting burned out and should pass the leadership to our faithful friends Bruce and Ella Samuelson. Our next leaders were Wilson and Jewel Leake, Dick and Sally Heuschkel , Jan Parr and now Bones and Connie Anderson. God has continued to bless this ministry and the Olympians continued to be a vital organization for the seniors in our church today.

The chorus that was dear to our hearts as we were leaving the ministry to seniors was the song " In His Time." Do you remember it?

> In His time, in His time,
> He makes all things beautiful in His time.
> Lord, please show me every day,
> As you're teaching me Your way,
> That You do just what You say, In Your time.
>
> In Your time, in Your time,
> You make all things beautiful in Your time.
> Lord my life to You I bring,
> May each song I have to sing.
> Be to You a lovely thing, In Your time."

During the time we were working with the Olympians, I also worked with the Northwest Assemblies of God Seniors Director, Rev. Merle Glew as our Olympic District Seniors Coordinator. I periodically wrote articles for him and collected articles from other churches in our area to be put in a Seniors Adult Ministry (SAM) Newsletter.

Because of this contact, he arranged for me to speak at a district meeting in Seattle, Washington and also one in Oregon, on how to form a seniors' ministry in the church. When we went to Oregon, Bruce and Ella Samuelson traveled with us and after I spoke for the meeting down there we drove on down to an oceanside, former motel that was being remodeled as a retreat center.

We were hoping it would be a good place for the Olympians to go in the future. It was real rough and we had to sleep in the same room with the Samuelson's. It was large enough, but not heated. Our beds were single, which didn't help much. That was one long trip that produced absolutely nothing for a future retreat for the Olympians, but the trip home was beautiful and we had such a great time with our friends, Bruce and Ella.

Then the Adult Ministries Consultant, William P. Campbell for the General Council of The Assemblies of God, contacted me to write an article to be published in their Advance magazine in May 1989. After I wrote the article, they asked me if the article could be enclosed in their packet offered to churches nationwide on how to start a Senior Adult Ministry. I was happy to have them use my method, in order that senior's within the church would be brought back into active fellowship.

Chapter 22

The Fordney's wanted to have another child as Meredith was now about three and they didn't want her to grow up without a sibling. Adopting a baby involved so much red tape and so many insurmountable hoops to jump that the quest seemed almost impossible. Although they lived in the state of Oregon, they made an application to an agency in Washington.

Usually, an agency from one state didn't adopt a child into another state. But just after Kevin and Nancy had completed their application, the Lord directed the Oregon caseworker to speak in a Washington high school, where a young pregnant girl was present. She contacted the caseworker and read the applications of several couples including Kevin and Nancy's and told the caseworker she wanted them as the parents of her child.

Even when it was considered unlikely, the Lord intervened and arrangements were made for Kevin and Nancy to adopt her baby when he was born. Matthew Robert was born March 10, 1986 in a Washington hospital and Kevin and Nancy were entrusted with the life of a sturdy little boy.

We were at Kathy and Dave's house when they brought him from the hospital to meet the family. He had a red-striped baseball sleeper on and he was so cute. We all were thrilled that Matthew was now part of our family.

Meredith had a brother who joined their family and not only bring someone for her to watch over but someone who returned her care with many a pinch, punch and kick. The Karate Kid himself. Boys are different from girls you know.

The following year Cindy and Bill announced to the family that they were expecting another child and we anxiously waited the big occasion. Cindy and Bill had just moved into their new house in Silverdale and Bill was still a submariner at Bangor. On August 23, 1987 Ashley Elizabeth Morris arrived at the Bremerton Naval Hospital weighing 10 pounds 6 ounces. It was a difficult delivery for Cindy and looking back the baby probably should have been delivered by "C" section.

Ashley was a large and happy baby who was slow at developing the usual skills of turning over and sitting up. A Naval doctor was treating her for asthma and Ashley just wasn't improving. So Cindy and I took her to a Port Orchard doctor recommended by Vickie Hopkins, Cindy's best friend, and the doctor found that Ashley had ear infections in both ears and pneumonia. Her doctor gave her antibiotics and cleared up her problems.

As soon as she was off the asthma medication, she rolled over and started to slowly develop the skills she should have been able to perform earlier. Ashley developed into a sweet, sensitive little girl who loved everyone and wanted to please.

As she grew, she loved to play and would rather run than eat. When I mention eat, I really wish I could say she had an appetite for what was good for her. But I'm afraid her main food was McDonald's McNuggets, pop, peanut butter, plain white bread and ice cream. When she ordered a hamburger she ordered it without the meat. No one could get her to even taste what she was not familiar with. But she still grew into a tall, slim lovely young lady and we thank God for her.

After over 30 years, Pastor Munger and Erika decided to resign as pastors of our church. We just couldn't imagine the church without their leadership. Glen was on the committee to hunt for an appropriate pastor and after a thorough search, the board decided we already had our next pastor on the pastoral staff, Marc Pearson.

What an easy change over we experienced and we were thrilled that Pastor and Erika could leave the church in such good hands. Pastor Marc had already been our Assistant Pastor for about eleven years and we were fortunate to maintain the same depth of teaching we had experienced.

Meanwhile, Pastor and Erika took their new vacation vehicle south and enjoyed the winter with other snowbirds that struggled through the nice warm weather and had to spend time on the golf course or relax under a palm tree. It didn't take Al long however, before he was busy ministering as a chaplain in a retirement facility.

The Munger's purchased a lovely desert home in a gated community and Glen and I were privileged to visit them for a potluck when they hosted three other couples from the Kitsap area. We also played putt-putt golf near their home with the group, even though the wind was blowing up a storm.

Chapter 23

"God blessed the seventh day, and sanctified it: because that in it He had rested from all His work which God created and made."

Genesis 2:3"

Probably every person who has ever had a job, whether it was teaching school, plowing a field, or raising a family, a time of rest is looked forward to with great expectations. One of the blessed things about growing old is that you have an excuse to sit down, get a cup of hot coffee, prop up your feet and take a rest. If you are lucky no one will disturb you and you can dream of the past or fantasize of the future.

In 1993 our son-in-law Bill Morris had served in the Navy 22 years and it was time for him to join the ranks of the retired. We received a nice invitation along with other family and friends to attend his retirement ceremony at Bangor Submarine Station. It was a grand occasion with a tour of the main buildings and a ceremony in the auditorium where those who were retiring were presented awards and commendations and then officially declared no longer to be a member of the active United States Submarine Forces.

Bill was an outstanding chief and I'm sure at Bangor they really missed him. But Bill's retirement at 42 years of age didn't qualify him to put his feet up and take a nap. He had a family to raise, a mortgage to pay and other hills to climb. Bill and Cindy lived so close to us and because he was a jack-of-all-trades, he could do and would do just about anything we called on him to do. Through the years he has gladly helped us many, many times when we needed his strength or expertise. I wouldn't be typing this book if he hadn't set me up on the computer and came to my rescue whenever I was in a bind. He is probably getting tired of me calling him and saying "Bill can you help me with "........." Thank you, Bill, you have been like a knight in shining armor to me all these years.

May of 1992 we celebrated 50 years of marriage and we wanted to have a fun time celebrating with family and friends. We had heard the Circuit Riders Quartet sing and play their instruments at our church and as we both liked country music we decided it would be different for our 50th to have a western barbecue with the quartet supplying the entertainment. We asked Jerry Arntz if he could help us plan the food for our celebration and he thought it would be a good idea if we'd come to their lovely Kingston home and he would cook a barbecue that he felt would be nice for the party. His choice of food was delicious and we gave him the go ahead for the menu. We also asked him to get several men he knew to help him with the cooking.

Our invitations were in keeping with the theme of western days, as we sent a "Wanted" sign on bright yellow paper that said "You Are Wanted" and a picture of Glen and myself all dressed up in western gear and the particulars of our 50th party.

Then I asked my dear friend Gail Stivers, who had helped me for several different occasions, to work her magic with the decorations and make the gym look like a real country barn setting.

The stage was erected with room dividers behind it and with tools, ropes etc hanging on the wall. She took bails of hay and scattered them around on the platform and put barrels, boxes and a milk can with a horse saddle to help establish the mood. Across the gym above the dinner tables she hung clothes such as petticoats, pants, dresses, blankets etc. to look like they were on the line drying. Each table had a red-checkered tablecloth and for table centerpieces lanterns, tools, old graniteware, pans, coffee pots and anything she could come up with to match the theme.

I made 30 apple and Marion berry pies and froze them for the dessert. On the day of the party I had about five women bake the pies and bring them to the kitchen steaming hot and ready to eat. Oh we were going to have a great party.

Kevin Fordney, our son-in-law was stable master and he did a wonderful job of recalling our 50 years of marriage. Besides our many church friends, some of our guests came from years gone by and people both Glen and I had worked with when we were in the working world.

Special guests were Karsten and Louise Solheim from Phoenix, Arizona who are the owners of Ping Golf Clubs. Although our invitation said "no gifts please" they brought both of us a Ping Zing 5 putter with our names and "50th Anniversary Wishes From Karsten & Louise" engraved on them.

The handout was a folder with a time line of 50 years of our married life. It had a picture of us shortly after we were married in 1942 on the front, inside pictures of the three girls with their husbands and kids and the time line of 50 years of our lives and on the back a picture of us taken in 1992. It said, "Things are used up, worn out, outgrown, out of style. Nothing seems to last for long. Nothing, that is except love and memories. A love that grows deeper with each passing year and precious memories of a God-given family drawn close to each other and to Him. Thank you for being a part of this special time of remembering 50 years of God's love and faithfulness. Glen & Shirley Odle May 2, 1992." Thank you God for giving us those wonderful years together.

Our friendship with Karsten and Louise Solheim has grown through the years. We first met Louise when Marge and I were living with Grandma and Grandpa LaDuke on their chicken ranch when we moved back home from California. Louise lived just across the Benson Highway from us and we had a lot of fun playing with her. As we grew up our ways parted but we never completely lost track of Louise. She was married, had a family and lived in California, back East, and then permanently in Arizona.

On one of our trips after visiting the folks in Tucson, Glen and I stopped in Phoenix and gave Louise a call. Being hospitable, she immediately invited us to come stay with them for a while and play some golf on their golf course at Moon Valley Country Club.

We accepted and were royally entertained. From then on, we stopped and stayed with them when we were in the area and were treated to all kinds of fun occasions. I remember that one time they were going to a formal musical and she told me to go into her guest closet and pick out a formal dress to wear. Fortunately, we wore the same size and I went in style. I don't know what they did for Glen but I know he was dressed appropriately.

One of their salesmen fit us both for a set of clubs during a later visit and what it cost us was only what they charged the professionals for their golf clubs. They also had the Ping clothing line and every time we visited the company store we got men's shirts and other items at a reduced cost.

On one occasion, Paul Harvey invited the Solheims to a special dinner at the Harvey's golf club while we were visiting Karsten and Louise, and we were included in the invitation. The other guests at a huge round table were doctors and businessmen and their wives who were hosted by Paul Harvey in order to familiarize them with the Mayo Clinic's new medical facilities being built in the Phoenix area.

We couldn't believe we were eating with the Harvey's and enjoying their company and not listening to him over the radio. We expected any minute that he would say "And that's the rest of the story."

In June of 1993, our oldest grandson Scott Schilperoort graduated from WF West High School in Chehalis and our seats were in the bleachers. Glen and I both hate bleacher seats and have difficulty climbing up those steps and sitting through a program without feeling like we would fall through the cracks.

For a graduation present we had decided to send Scott to Focus on the Family camp for graduating high school seniors in Colorado Springs, Colorado. It was a wonderful trip for him and he came back so enthused with the theme of the camp, "World view versus the Christian view." He was all ready to become a politician after that camp and he enrolled in Western Washington University in Bellingham and graduated from there in December 1997. Several jobs later, he is now employed in

Bellevue and using his knowledge and speaking skills in persuading auto owners to use the services of the body shop he represents. That's kind of like being a politician isn't it?

In 1994 we received an official letter from the Ping Golf Manufacturing Company inviting us to play in the Professional Amateur Tournament of the Ping Golf Cellular One LPGA Championship at the Columbia Edgewater Country Club in Portland, Oregon. It gave all the particulars in the letter of how to enroll to play in the tournament and with the completed application we were to send a sizable sum of money in the thousands of dollars. We had played at expensive courses before, but none that expensive. I called Louise and told her we had received the letter and thanked her for the invitation but couldn't play in the tournament, as we could not afford the fee. She laughed and said, that's all right they'd pay for us.

So we sent our application in and our sponsor was Ping Golf Manufacturing Company. The day of the Pro/AM we were issued a badge and were placed on different teams with four amateurs and one lady professional each. We played best ball, and if you don't know how it goes, the pro plays her own ball and the four amateurs play a scramble. In a scramble each player tees off and then the best drive is selected and all four players hit from that spot.

After each shot the group chooses the best shot and everyone plays from there, until the hole is completed. I'll never forget how I felt when I teed off. Think of standing up there with a crowd of spectators quietly watching you and four teammate strangers, one of them a lady professional, and have the announcer say "Shirley Odle playing for Ping Golf Clubs out of Rolling Hills Golf Club in Bremerton, Washington." Thank goodness they didn't give my average score as I'm sure I was playing because Louise was my friend, not that I was a good golfer.

Deathly quiet and all eyes on me, I took a swing at the ball. Now that's pressure. In spite of the pressure I had a great time, as some of the men were just as wild as I was. However, there was a time in the eighteen holes that my ball was the "best ball." My group didn't come out on the top or anywhere near it, but everyone was a winner. We all were given so many wonderful gifts from the sponsors that when we both walked back to our car we could hardly carry the loot. Rain gear, a golf club, a basket of fruit, golf shoes, and our first cell phones and on and on. That was my first experience with a cell phone and I have used one up until the present and I still I don't know how they work. If someone calls I try my best to answer them.

In the clubhouse they had a VIP Lounge for participants in the event where we could relax and eat or drink whatever we wanted at no cost. Now that's how the rich and famous live.

We have also stayed in one of the Solheim's lovely condos on their short nine-hole course for a week and they took us out to eat nearly every evening, either to the clubhouse or a nice restaurant. We were also entertained in their lovely home situated between the 10th tee and 18th final hole across from the Moon Valley Club House. They have been wonderful friends and I wish we could have been givers instead of only takers all these years. Louise is now living in a lovely condominium and it makes me hesitate to communicate with her as she would invite me to stay with her and I feel I'm imposing.

Chapter 24

The economy in 1995 was doing fine. New houses were being built at a rapid pace. We were contemplating selling the big house and putting a smaller bungalow on the acre of land we bought from my brother Bob. We had heard about the wonderful quality of the prefab modular homes that were being built in the south Tacoma area and then transported to a prepared building site.

We drove down to the display houses and viewed the various models and immediately fell in love with the Tiffany III plan that had everything we wanted in a small home. We put $2,000.00 down on the price given which left a balance of $97,465.45. When the house was on site they would build a 24 x 24 garage attached to the back of the house for an additional $11,421.74. Now all we needed to do was to sell our original home and we'd be in a new little home.

I started a thorough house cleaning and put everything in the basement of the house we hoped to sell and preceded as though we were moving into the new house. At the same time we put our house on the market, housing sales slowed up and we had few who were even interested.

One day I got a call from the president of the Evergreen Modular Homes, Inc. and he said he and his manager wanted to come out and talk to us about our home. We made an appointment for Sunday afternoon for their visit not knowing what to expect. When they came we showed them our home and then over coffee and cookies sat down to serious conversation.

The president of Evergreen Modular Homes said sales had started to soften and he wanted to maintain his experienced work force by keeping them busy building houses. He wanted to offer us a deal. A wonderful deal that blew us over. They would build our home, put it on our lot and we could move into it without paying anything until the original house sold. We couldn't believe our ears and wanted to see it in writing before we said yes. Things just don't happen that way in the real world.

Shortly after that opportunity, I was having a moving sale when a young lady came in who was house sitting in a home down the beach. She wanted to see our house. I was busy with customers so told her to go upstairs and look around and feel free to make herself at home. It wasn't long before she returned to the basement and said she and her husband wanted to buy the place. What a surprise. The Lord had sold our house for us and arranged for us to have our new home delivered on our lot without paying anymore than our original $2,000.00 down payment. What a great God we serve.

Our real estate lady was notified, as well as the builder of our modular home. Things started to move quickly and it wasn't long before I was looking out our bedroom window watching the big truck jockey the little yellow bungalow onto its footings. I think nearly all the neighborhood was also interested in that procedure. As soon as the house was securely attached to the footings the workmen began to build the garage on the back of the house. The addition of the garage made an interesting "L" configuration in our back yard and we had a deck and concrete patio built in that space by Jim Ray a young man who went to our church.

This time, instead of Glen doing all the landscaping, we had Karen Page who owned Landshapes Gardens, put in shrubs and perennials in the front and sides of our new home. Vern's Top Soil brought in soil that would serve as a foundation for the seed that Danson's Hydro Seeding would blow in from a huge truck that simplified planting the lawn. All Glen had to do was rent a roller and keep the lawn area both wet and solidly seated. Kitsap Paintsmith painted everything that needed to be painted on the garage and front and back decks and our little home was the new jewel of the neighborhood.

Glen bought a bright blue standing propane heater and had it installed in the front room and with wallpaper and rugs the little bungalow was now ready for occupancy. Bill Morris had a friend of his from the submarine base help move us in and we were happily moved from the big house to our nice warm little new home.

Chapter 25

On February 19, 2000 Glen celebrated his 80th birthday in the West Wing of the new building of Christ Memorial Church and we had a wonderful time remembering many happy years with friends and family. At the same time, our second grandson, Jason Schilperoort, graduated from George Fox University and opened up his office in the Beaverton, Oregon area, selling cutlery for CutCo. He did well and learned a lot about being a salesman and employer in the business world.

In June of 2001 both Jennifer and Meredith graduated from high school. We attended Jennifer's awards ceremony in the Central Kitsap High School and were surprised at the number of scholarships awarded to the graduates. We were impressed that the Methodist Church gave a nice scholarship to one of their young people and Glen and I wondered and talked together about why our church did not have such a program.

It was a source of prayer and we continued to consider it when we went to Sky Valley, California where my brother Bob and Ailene had a nice vacation home. We had rented what we thought was a nice mobile home in the same park, but one day when I was in the bathroom, I noticed a mouse playing around on the floor and going in and out under the door. Then I began to see cockroaches in various places and a granddaddy sized one in my garbage nearly scared me to death. I told Glen I was thinking of moving up to Bob and Ailene's place, as I couldn't stand all those cockroaches.

When I got into bed that night and pulled up my covers a big cockroach ran up my arm. I screamed so loud and Glen came running into the bedroom just in time to see me catapult out of bed shaking all over. That was the end of our stay in that place. We packed all our stuff and moved up to Bob and Ailene's modular that night. When we got there I called the Crosses in Turlock and told them we had moved into their vacation home.

When we returned home from our California vacation, we arranged to meet with the board of our church to present the possibility of organizing a scholarship program for the high school graduates of our church. The board thought it was a good idea and Tom Duchemin met with us to help with the planning. The result was that a scholarship board was formed with Richard Tizzano as chairman and Bruce Samuelson, Bill Lomas, Wes Davis our Youth Director, and Glen and I to finalize the board.

All of these men were members of long standing in our church except Richard Tizzano, who with his wife and baby were new to our church from California. Richard, a member of the Scholarship Board of the Rotary Club expressed his interest in helping us with the formation of our organization.

Conrad Green looked into the legal aspects of the plan and we were off and running with the first application in 2003 and a $1,000.00 scholarship presented to Bethany Tyler. A total of 25 students have been awarded scholarships amounting to $21,525.00. What a joy to see these young people blessed by this scholarship, which is now appropriately named the Glen Odle Scholarship.

Our grandkids were growing up and we saw a lot of happy occasions. The first being Jason Schilperoort and Ginger Kooristra announcing their wedding to be held in the refurbished ferry terminal in Bellingham on September 22, 2002. Unfortunately, I was recovering from a heart attack and we were not able to attend. However, we did attend the wedding of Jennifer Morris and Jason Pawlak on September 7, 2003 in the Bremerton Eagles' outdoor gazebo overlooking Dyes Inlet. Seeing both couples happily married and in their homes was such an answer to prayer.

The next big happening was the birth of a new addition to our family. Jason Pawlak's folks were raising dogs in Texas and their red male Pomeranian and female Cockapoo had four little black puppies on our anniversary in 2004.

Jason's folks were coming to see Jennifer and Jason when the pups were about eight weeks old, and we asked them to bring a little black female to us when they came. What a darling little ball of mischief. When they brought her to our home, Mitzi just ran from one person to the other. Our large backyard was just perfect for her and she loved to romp and roll in the soft green grass.

Her little teeth were like needles though and she chewed everything she came upon including my hearing aides. I had to purchase new ones and they cost over $5,000.00, which raised the price for Mitzi considerably. Glen loved her and she was so much company for him. At that time he was having trouble with his hip and did a lot of sitting with Mitzi on his lap. Most of his sweaters were minus the buttons and parts of the pockets.

She was so naughty and caused so many problems that at one time we thought we'd have to give her away. I did a lot of crying when someone came to look at her. I could hardly tell them about her, I was crying so hard. It was like giving one of our kids away. Finally, Glen couldn't endure all my crying and said we probably should keep her. Whoopee, was I ever happy. But looking back I'm so glad we did keep her as we found out that with patience and training she would outgrow the puppy stage and develop into a loving happy dog. She is now seven years old and my constant companion, greeting most of my visitors with a burst of wiggles and joy. Everyone loves Mitzi here at Crista Shores Apartments, except a very few people who fear they'll fall over her leash and break a leg or hip.

In 2004 Matt Fordney graduated from high school in Vancouver, Washington and the next year Ashley Morris finished high school at Central Kitsap here in Silverdale. Meredith also finished up her schooling at Seattle Pacific and made arrangements to live with some girl friends in the Los Angeles area, in order to get a job working in the TV industry. She got a job in a high-class furniture store to help pay for her rent and other expenses and followed up leads until she was hired for a job in TV casting.

In the fall of 2006 the economy continued to boom. Houses were selling at top prices and Dave, who was working for Century 21 suggested we take advantage of the prices and put our new little house up for sale. What a pain to sell that beautiful house that was just right for us. The Lord was evidently moving us to another phase in our lives.

Years ago we had considered moving into Crista Shores Retirement Facility but Glen said he would not go there, as the places were too small. But now he was suffering more and more with his hip and could hardly get around. We got him a scooter and the carpenters building two new houses in the lots behind us, built him a ramp to help Glen get from the garage into the house. But keeping up our acre of property was getting to be too much for both of us, so selling seemed the smart thing to do. Reluctantly, we had Dave put up a "for sale" sign in our front yard and almost before he had the sign post in the ground, a young lady who worked at Bangor stopped and asked to see the place. We told her to have her real estate dealer contact Dave and in a few short transactions our home was sold at top price. Now we'd see what the Lord had for us this time.

The family time on Christmas that year was wonderful. We drove to the Schilperoorts on December 22nd and spent Saturday and Sunday. Scott and Jason and their dad were the cooks on Saturday night and the menu was the usual clam chowder and deep fried shrimp. Scott was the all time winner, eating a gazillion shrimp and Jason and Glen came in as close seconds. After dinner we had a time of celebration and opening gifts on Saturday night. That was the time gifts to each other were opened. Jason and Ginger surprised us with a small blue album. When we opened it, it had an inscription on the cover that read BABY. It took a while for it to sink in that we were expecting our first great-grandchild. What a wild time of celebration that we were soon to have a baby in our family.

Then before we left on Christmas morning to go to the Fordney's for the "all family celebration" we had to see what Santa had left in our huge stockings hanging around the wood stove in the family room.

Kathy always got so many interesting gifts for everybody that she had accumulated whenever she saw something to her liking.

After opening our Christmas socks, we hurriedly bundled up as the weather had changed to a steady rain. The wind was blowing too and we were glad when the trip down I-5 ended at the lovely home of Nancy and Kevin's. They had their large home decorated so beautifully and everyone was excited to be together as a family. All except Jennifer and Jason who were stationed on Guam, seeing how the people there celebrated their holiday. We had our usual Christmas dinner fit for the royal family and Meredith and Ashley played Santa and passed out the gifts. Glen got a watch he'd wanted, along with other things he had on his Christmas list. The crowning gift for both of us was a digital camera with developer and supplies to accomplish the task of recording our families many activities. What an exciting gift that we would be able to enjoy for many years to come.

The time at the Fordney's was cut short as the buyer of our lovely little home on Beach Drive wanted to move in as soon after Christmas as possible. So we drove back to Kathy's that evening and then I drove us home to Poulsbo on Tuesday morning. It was a wet and hazardous trip and when we finally reached our place, we were happy to have made it.

Chapter 26

We had no idea what lay ahead of us as we unpacked the car and took our Christmas gifts into the front room and placed them under the Christmas tree, I noticed above the propane stove there was a wet spot on the edge of the soffit. On closer examination I discovered the reason for the spot was that some place water from the pouring rain must had gotten in under the roof's shingles. I was so worried as our buyer wanted to take possession in a couple of days.

I called Mark Ross immediately and he came right over to see if he could find the leak. It was still pouring down rain, so Mark couldn't get out on the roof, but he felt one of his laborers could open up the area and fix it in about two hours. Being the holiday season, everyone was on vacation and he had no one to fix it immediately, so he planned to communicate with the buyer and fix it after she moved in.

Wednesday, all the gang came to the house, and like a whirlwind they packed boxes, moving some to the Wertz's basement for storage, and the rest they moved into our new apartment at Crista Shores. Glen and I were really in the way during the move and we attempted to escape being trampled.

I had made arrangements for the crew to eat at Crista Shores dining room and at five o'clock we all met there for a quick delicious meal. Dave had rented a truck and had to get it back at a prearranged time, so I think he and Kevin missed out on most of their dinner. You wouldn't believe how fast they got the apartment whipped into shape. It was amazing. Not that we knew where things were, but they were in the apartment and put on shelves or in drawers. From then on we'd have to play the game of "find the right shelf or drawer." When they were all finished, our apartment looked so attractive and we were thrilled to be there.

We had had Mitzi with Gail and Mary Lou Tigner since the 20th of December so she didn't get to experience all the excitement. Mitzi stayed with them until March the 30th when both Gail and Mary Lou got a bug and I had to get Mitzi and take her to our new apartment. After a week I was able to find care for her at Eileen Walbourn's in Kingston. Mitzi adjusted quickly there as Eileen had a small dog "Sadie" who was really happy to welcome Mitzi into her domain. They soon became best of pals running in the fenced yard and chasing the squirrels. We were not able to have Mitzi with us in our second floor apartment, as dogs are not allowed above the Beach Level. The apartments on the beach level have sliding glass doors and access to the outside for pet potty breaks and walks. Our name was put on the waiting list for a two-bedroom beach level apartment and when one became available we could move in and have Mitzi with us again.

The day for Glen's hip surgery was approaching fast. He had some misgivings, but he decided if he was to get back to walking normally and possibly playing golf again, he would have to give it a try. Kathy took us on January 17th for the pre-op appointment and it was determined that an echogram would be necessary the day before the surgery because of a heart murmur that was detected.

On the 23rd of January we were back with Kathy for the echogram at the University of Washington Medical Center and then we checked into Hotel Nexis where Glen would stay with us for only one night before the operation. Early the next morning Glen was admitted into the surgery pavilion and we were able to go in with him while he was waiting for his call to surgery. That was a long day and we spent it first with him and then all day in the room provided for family members waiting for surgery results. The facilities for family were first class. However no meals were served, just coffee or tea. But we had eaten breakfast provided by the hotel and then got all our other meals from the hospital cafeteria.

Dr. Manner finally came into talk to us explaining that all had gone well and that we could visit Glen in ICU when they got him up there. We were riding on cloud nine and were so happy. Glen did fine each day, but he was slow progressing to the point where he could be released from the hospital into therapy. Finally, on the 31st a cabulance took him to Northwood Lodge in Silverdale and Kathy drove our car to the nursing facility. It was late that night before we got there and an orderly admitted Glen.

The next day, I had a doctor's appointment because I had developed shingles and Dr. Carlton had to treat me with several medications. He assured me I would be over the shingles quickly and I'd never have them again. So far he is right and I am so thankful I didn't suffer as much as so many people do.

When we got back to Northwood, I found out Glen had been taken to Harrison Hospital because of a blood clot in his lung and a filter was put on his heart to keep any more clots from lodging there. He also had developed a bleeding ulcer, so they were unable to give him blood thinners to stop future clots.

It was necessary for him to stay in the hospital until Sunday the 4th. Then, would you believe it, Northwood had a lock down because of a flu problem, so instead of going back to Northwood he had to go to Belmont Nursing Facility which was just a couple of blocks from the hospital. Things just seemed to be deteriorating, but at that time I wasn't aware that we were on a downward spin. Glen was put way down the hall, alone in a room, where no one seemed to venture and I was really upset about that. He was supposed to be getting therapy and only when I complained did they start. Glen was at Belmont until the 8th of February, when Kathy came up to take us to the University of Washington Medical Center to take the stitches out. Dr. Manner was confident that all would be well and he set up another appointment for the 8th of March.

When we went home that night, Glen was admitted back into Northwood in a private room that was very comfortable for him. It was a large room with a couple of chairs and a lovely settee with a coffee table, nice little refrigerator, microwave and large private bath.

Northwood is considered one of the best nursing and therapy facilities in the northwest. They treat their patients super and the therapy machines and equiptment are top of the line.

A special kitchen is maintained just off of what they call the Fireside Room, where visitors and patients can meet and enjoy the cookies, fruit, punch, coffee, cappuccino, hot chocolate, and ice cream provided for them. We had Glen's 87th birthday there with Marge and Phil, Cindy, Bill and Ashley, Jane and Al Martin all sharing his birthday cake with him.

As Glen progressed in his therapy, I had to learn how to get him up, put him in his wheel chair, get him in the car etc. I spent every day there from morning until time to go back to Crista for my dinner. He was looking great and we fully expected him to come home and be able to enjoy the plans we'd made for continued progress in walking and being normal again. We even had an appointment with a special shoe manufacturer to make a shoe with a lift that would also add stability.

Glen had two doctor's appointments. One on March 5th when he was taken by van from Northwood to see Dr. Yee, and the next day to Dr. Bilsten to have a belly catheter put on, readying him for going home to Crista Shores. Kathy came up on Thursday the 8th for his visit to Dr. Manner's office at the Roosevelt Center of UW Medical Center and we followed the route we had taken so many times before. Glen was officially checked out of Northwood and things were looking good for him.

It was a long hard day and we missed the five P.M. ferry from Seattle on the way home and had to wait an hour on the pier for the next one. It was dark when we got over on the West side of Puget Sound and drove toward Silverdale. Kathy and I stopped at a Chinese take-out to get something for all of us to eat. When we got home Glen said he was too tired to eat, so I got him to bed and we had our dinner. After dinner Kathy went home to be with Dave for the weekend.

During the night, Glen complained of a stomach ache. He had a terrible night and he was exhausted by morning. I called the doctor and was told that probably because he'd been taking antibiotics some kind of a reaction occurred and caused the diarrhea, so I should give him Pepto-Bismol and Imodium. Of course I had to go to the store to get the medicine and I didn't dare leave Glen alone, so I called Cindy and Bill to come to our place. Bill was a lifesaver. He helped Glen and took care of him when I went to the drug store.

When I got home there had been a noticeable change in Glen's facial appearance. Around his eyes the skin surface was blue and he was staring ahead. When I waved my hand in front of his face he didn't change expressions. I told Bill to call 911 as I thought Glen had had a stroke. Then I asked him to talk, smile, lift both arms (tests to see if a person has had a stroke) and he could do it all. When the medics arrived, they knew he needed immediate care and transported him to the hospital emergency in Bremerton.

When Bill and I got there, they had him in ER working on him. We were able to be with him and spoke to the doctors about what was going on. His heart was okay, blood pressure stable and they hadn't a clue why he was so sick. They told us he was going down and was in the process of dying.

I couldn't believe it, he had been doing so well. The emergency nurse moved him from ER to ICU and on the way there he looked up and said, "Oh, It's beautiful." The nurse asked him "what's beautiful Glen?" and he didn't answer. Then they hooked him up to all the proper apparatus, oxygen, IV, etc. and about one a.m. Bill took me home to rest. Early the next morning I talked to Glen on the phone and he sounded fine to me. By the time I got to the hospital he was on life support and he never spoke to me again. Another doctor came in that morning and suggested we had three options. Do nothing and just let him die, operate and not find the problem, or operate and maybe they could find the problem and fix it. We chose to have them operate to see if they could fix it. It took them so long to get him ready for surgery. It was noon before they finally took him to the operating room. Bill and I had settled in for a long wait. But in 30 to 45 minutes they were back with him and put him back in ICU. The doctor took us into a small private room and said that Glen's bowels were all dead from lack of blood.

Evidently a blood clot was in the main artery to the bowel and because the blood had stopped circulating there, it had died. Lack of blood for 24 hours made the bowel black and lacking in elasticity. His suggestion was to call the family and they would keep him on life-support until they arrived, so we could all say our goodbyes. I was prepared for this as I saw how deathly ill he was.

The girls were shocked when we called them. Nancy and Kevin picked up Kathy and were at the hospital around four p.m. Dave had a house to show, so he would come up later. The doctor briefed us on what they would do when we were ready to remove his life support. They would put a morphine shot into his IV to keep him comfortable and then remove the breathing tube and all life support. The doctor said he might struggle for breath and that it might take two to four hours or overnight for him to die. After all that Glen had endured and how well he was when he came home from his last check up at the University of Washington Medical Center, it didn't seem possible that he would actually be dying.

Richard Tizzano visited right before we went through this procedure and also Ken and Grace Lindgren and Pastor Marc and Carol Pearson. The Lord's timing was perfect. What a blessing to have the support of those who had supported us for so many years.

We had a nice time of prayer and they left so that the family could be alone with Glen. Most of the time Bill knelt praying and held Glen's hand quietly. We each told Glen how much we loved him and what he'd meant to us. When we were ready, the proper doctor put the shot in the IV and all systems were shut off. We watched the red line on the monitor slowly go down to a straight line.

Glen didn't struggle, nor did he have any kind of reaction, only just slipped away to Jesus. It took just twenty minutes for the whole process. From corruptible to eternal life. From a miserable existence to joyful wholeness again.

Glen didn't have the opportunity to enjoy our move to Crista Shores, or be able to walk normally again, or play golf as he so dearly wanted. But he moved into the mansion prepared for him and walked the streets of gold and was greeted by all those gone on before. He has heard the heavenly music and joined them in their songs and feasted on the fruit from the tree of life. Best of all, the Lord Jesus Christ has called him by his new name and introduced him to the Father. Well done good and faithful servant, enter into your reward.

Chapter 27

The Celebration Service was held at Christ Memorial Church with the help of so many faithful family and friends. Pastor Marc Pearson directed the service with our Chaplain Steve Reiland from Crista Shores reciting scripture and praying before the congregation sang, "Great is Thy Faithfulness." Brett Youngquist, Glen's great-nephew sang "How Great Thou Art." Karen Trostad spent many hours arranging a beautiful media presentation of Glen's life journey. Then our sons-in-law, Dave and Kevin, along with grandsons Jason and Scott paid tribute to Glen and reflected on his life.

Two congregational songs "What a Friend We Have in Jesus" and "There's Something About That Name" were sung and four men from the church spoke about their particular experiences with Glen during his life in the church. Bruce Samuelson on the Olympians, Frank Burlingame director of the Music Department, Conrad Green on the Board of Elders and Richard Tizzano the Scholarship Committee, all gave tribute to Glen. Merle Trostad sang Glen's favorite song "Daystar" just before Pastor Pearson delivered a message of hope. Pastor also announced that the youth scholarship program would be named "The Glen Odle Scholarship." The service was closed with the congregation singing "'Tis So Sweet to Trust in Jesus." The organist was Frank Burlingame and pianist Dianne Johnston.

A large number of friends attended the reception, beautifully hosted by the Women of Christ Memorial Church in the Pearson Fellowship Hall. After the reception, the family left for a private viewing at Cherry

Grove Chapel before the burial in the cemetery plot next to our best friends, Rollin and Doris Michelsen. Many of our close friends and family were in attendance including Jennifer and Jason Pawlak from Guam. Glen would have been so overwhelmed if he had been there for that celebration. He always thought that he just didn't measure up to what he wanted to be and I was so happy for each person who acknowledged his true worth.

Chapter 28

Two and a half months after Glen passed away, Kathy arranged a trip for me with the three girls on the Golden Princess sailing to Alaska. Kathy and Nancy roomed together and I roomed with Cindy, as this was Cindy's first cruise ship experience and she was a little uneasy. What a wonderful trip we had and the weather was beautiful in Alaska.

Even in Ketchikan, where it usually rains the sun was shining. What fun the four of us had trying on the expensive fur coats and funny miners hats in the department stores. Pictures and memories will long keep that lovely time we had together as a family fresh in our minds.

In November of 2007, I got word that the apartment I had walked by so many times and asked the Lord for, was going to be vacated. I wasn't the only one waiting for a two-bedroom apartment on the beach area and I anxiously waited for word if I was the one to get it. Well you know the Lord is faithful and it wasn't long before Ashley's friend Daniel and his twin brother Ken moved me from the second floor, down to the beach level to that lovely apartment.

Crista Shores was in the beginning of a great refurbishing of the exterior of our building and a cocoon covered the waterside for nearly a year to protect workers and the area being worked on from the elements. It was difficult to see out of the apartments and impossible to go out on the balcony as they had been removed and the area tightly covered with fabric.

I could now have my dog with me and it was an adjustment for her to move from Lee Mae Elkin's place, where she was loved and cared for, for at least a year. But I was really glad to have Mitzi's company again, as did others here in our retirement community. Every day on her walk around the building she would greet each person with her waggley tail.

In February of 2008, Kathy and I flew to Sacramento and rented a car and drove to Bob and Ailene's place to visit for a few days. Ailene had a special dinner and invited all their family and it was so great to see how the kids had developed and grown into responsible adults.

Then Kathy and I drove to San Francisco and stayed in a hotel, just doors from the hotel where Glen and I had stayed when we were married. We bought a pass for the cable cars and spent a couple of days exploring the great city of San Francisco. You know the song "I lost my heart in San Francisco." Well Glen and I sang that song for years as our favorite, secret lovey-dovey song.

The wind was cold by the water and I gladly exchanged the jacket I got in Alaska, for a warmer one with a hood, that had a San Francisco logo on it. We used our cable car pass to go all over the city, even out to Golden Gate Park and by the time our visit was over we were worn out. Leann and Barry picked us up at the airport when we checked our car in and drove us to their house in Rancho Cordova. On Sunday we went to church with them. It was such a big, beautiful church and I enjoyed taking pictures inside of all they had to offer for their members. We stayed two nights there and enjoyed their hospitality before they drove us back to the airport to board our plane back to Portland, Oregon. What a great time we had visiting family and friends.

In July 2008 the long awaited great-grandchild arrived. I was wondering if I'd ever live to see the day I'd be blessed with one. But on Nancy's birthday on July 20th 2008, Madelyn Lou Schilperoort was born to Jason and Ginger. From the start she was a darling and I wish you could have seen how Dave and Kathy smothered her with love. It was so wonderful to see. Thank you, Lord for blessing us with children. For several years we thought we would be childless, but He has increased our union of two to fifteen and counting. Praise the Lord.

In October 2008, Bob invited me on the trip of a lifetime and Kathy was the only one in our family available to go with me. We flew to

New York, where we met Bob and Ailene before boarding an American Airline Flight to Barcelona, Spain.

When we got there, we took a van from the airport to our hotel and met the rest of our group there. Ailene's two sisters and their husbands had already checked into the hotel as they had taken a different airline across the United States than Bob and Ailene.

That evening we got directions to where the nice restaurants were and proceeded to find one. The main streets of the city are separated with a wide island in the middle planted with trees and where there was plenty of space for temporary tent shops to be set up at night. They sold various items, such as produce, breads, candy, knick-knacks, and clothing. Bob bought some almond candy for a treat and the rest of us raised the hopes of many other vendors as we strolled by their tent shops.

The Spanish people are great family people. We met many couples pushing their young children or babies in strollers, who were headed to storefront shops where their children were cared for during the evening. They also had many stores along the streets that specialized in children's toys, books or clothing and you could see where their interest was centered.

We finally all decided on the same restaurant and made our first attempt at ordering off a Spanish menu. A young waiter who had gone to school in the United States helped us make our choices. I loved watching all the people eat their dinner so differently from how we ate. They probably enjoyed watching us eat our dinner too.

The next day was a free day and after a nice breakfast in our hotel, we all got ready for a trip to see the sights in Barcelona. Several of us lasted only a block and then turned back to rest and enjoy the day before the cruise. I was one of those that didn't even last a block. A trip down to the lobby was all I took before turning back to snuggle into my bed again. I enjoyed reading a book and when the adventurous returned and told of the wonderful sights, I was sorry I had not gone. But you can be sure I didn't miss my experience of boarding that wonderful ship that would take us all around the upper Mediterranean down to Malta and up the boot of Italy and back to Spain.

The Norwegian Gem got under way at seven P.M. after waving goodbye to those who had come to see the ship slowly move out of the harbor. Kathy and I enjoyed a welcome barbecue on the activities deck and then snooped around to see what we would dare try to accomplish later on the trip. We watched a young man climb a rock tower and both Kathy and I decided we'd skip that one. To tell the truth there wasn't much in activities we did, as we were so busy sightseeing during the day and eating so grandly at night that such things as sliding down a water slide or soaking in the hot tub was not on our agenda. Besides, we had to keep from getting our hair wet.

The ship was a simply beautiful ship. Every deck was an adventure in its self. Each dining room had different levels of appropriate dress except the 24-hour cafeteria where you could get anything your tummy yearned for no matter what you had on. But you had to sanitize your hands as you came in the door to protect everyone from unwanted germs. They had a funny, happy guy there at the door that joked with everyone as they entered and made the procedure less trying.

The entertainment was first class and as we went through the casino, going from one area to the other, we noticed not many people were in there. After the shows in the evening we strolled through the ship's stores and looked at all the beautiful clothes, jewelry, and souvenirs. We usually went to bed at a reasonable time, as we had to get up early every day and eat our breakfast before meeting our van driver for our sightseeing trip.

Ailene had made contact with a family organization in Italy who had eight-passenger vans that met us at every stop, but Malta and Nice, France and gave us a personalized tour of each area and city. As we were using vans they were able to get us through the little streets and country farm areas where others with a bus couldn't venture.

Luncheon was ordered for us so we could taste a variety of Italian foods. I didn't have even one slice of pizza. At the end of the day when we got back to the ship our driver gave us the bill and we all paid the same, something like $75.00 to $100.00 dollars a day. The only exception was when our guide took us to a special gelato café, by a river in Florence, where we all ordered and paid for whatever appealed most to us.

Because they did not operate their agency on Malta, we took a double-decker bus there right from the ship to the tourist area, where hand blown glass articles were made and sold and then we drove around the island to visit the scenic areas. From Malta our ship went to Naples, and our guide drove us to Pompeii. A woman guide gave us a walking tour up the stone streets to the areas of destruction. That tour was a trying and tedious day for me and I decided that I would stay on the ship the next day, while the others went to Rome and Vatican City. Kathy had a fit and did her best to persuade me to go with the group. Finally after taking a nap I decided to go and on getting home the next day I realized it would have been terrible to be so close to that beautiful city and not to have seen it. There was more to see in Rome and the Vatican City than any of the other places we visited.

When we first got to Rome, we stopped for lunch before driving to the Vatican and waiting in line to enter the city. Our guide fit us with a communication device so she could keep in contact with us and we followed her through the various places of interest. St. Peter's Basilica was breathtaking with the interior walls and ceilings of the buildings beautifully painted with various scenes from the Bible. Statues and paintings of the struggles between Satan and Jesus, as well as angelic beings were everywhere and we followed our guide up stairs and down stairs, from building to building in a maze of people who were also following their guide.

When we came out into the square where the Pope usually addressed the people just before we exited the city, we couldn't find Bob. He could not be reached on his pager and we were all trying to remember when we had seen him last. The Vatican is so vast there is no way you can find a lost person. So after a thorough search of the last area we had visited, we decided to get in the van and go back to the ship without Bob.

When we got back to the ship Ailene waited at the gangplank for Bob and he finally reached the ship with his taxi driver driving at break-neck speed. The driver had called the captain of our ship and told him he had Bob and would be five minutes late. The ride put him back $150.00 but it was well worth it.

Our first stop for the next day was Pisa and the large area where the leaning tower was situated. Kathy and I tried to take pictures showing us holding up the tower. We weren't very successful with the picture, but at least it looked as though we were holding up the tower. Then on to a working olive estate, with trees older than we were.

Just before we reached Florence, our guide took us to a square, high and looking over Florence he gave us an interesting talk about the city. A choir, made up of young priests, were singing acappella in the square and their voices were so crystal clear and beautiful. What timing that we would be there at the same time.

This square was bustling with activity. Amateur painters were diligently working on the scene spread out before us, and in the center of the area was a statue of David. People were taking pictures from every position. A small café was also just off to the side, where people were sitting at tables, drinking a cup of coffee or just soaking up the sunshine in that beautiful place. I bought two small paintings from a young lady who was in the process of painting them and I had them framed when we reached home.

The ship stopped next in Nice, France and Kathy and I took a tour bus around Nice viewing many mansions hanging on the sides of the mountain cliffs. When we finally reached Monte Carlo, we disembarked the bus and puffed up the hill to the Casino. The view was breath taking and the landscape so lovely on that craggy peak above the Mediterranean. The casino wasn't open, but we didn't care, as we had not intended on wagering any of our money.

We did visit Princess Grace's garden and her palace, where the guards were walking sentry. Earlier we had seen the area on a treacherous road where Princess Grace had lost her life. We also could look down on the harbor and see the luxury yachts. During the annual Grand Prix car race it costs $50,000 a day to dock at the same marina. On the ship that night we celebrated my 86th birthday with a cake and a gift from our group of an official laminated map of the Mediterranean and the route our cruise ship would take, signed by our captain. The card on the gift was printed in either Italian or French and it says "Heureux Anniversaire" and inside

"Passe une yournee inoubliable." I also have a couple of pieces of frosting still left from the cake that I put in my photo album.

We arrived in Seattle the next day in the evening and I was so tired from the flights from Barcelona to New York and then to Seattle that we had to get a hotel in town for the night and take the ferry home to Bainbridge Island the next day. What a perfectly wonderful trip. We never could have gone if Bob hadn't asked us. I keep thinking Glen would have enjoyed that trip so much but maybe he's thinking the same about me and the trips and sights he's enjoying in the realms above.

On arriving home we were on a high that was hard to come down from. My baggage remained packed for several days and I couldn't face that task or any other task, I was so wound up. But I had to face reality and get on with my life here in busy Crista Shores. I had my dog to get and bring home as she had been at the Elkins for two weeks, having a wonderful time with their four dogs.

I had to get back to bowling on the Wii Team, finishing the eighteen knitted hats I was making for Christmas and playing Hand and Foot several nights a week. Oh yes, I have much to do besides being a part of this big family I have chosen to live with. I thank the Lord for allowing me to live here in my lovely apartment, in peace and safety with friends all around me, who care about me. When I have a bad day, some are quick to offer their help and share prayers, and when I have good news, many celebrate with me. Sadly, I have to bid farewell to some as they leave to enter their mansion above. But the separation is only temporary, as we who live and enjoy each day the Lord gives us here will also be joining them all as we sing praises around the throne in that beautiful land where we'll never be sick or never grow old.

Chapter 29

Finally, in spite of my stubborn resistance to Him, God has been with me, never leaving or forsaking me. He has patiently drawn me to Himself and planned my days and they were good. Oh, I haven't escaped the pains and problems of life, but God who is my healer, sustainer, rock, lover, and daily friend makes the path joyful in sorrow and peaceful in trial. Thank you, Jesus for not giving up on me.

All my life I have known the call of God and I resisted many times because I was afraid I'd have to spend my life in Africa or doing something I didn't want to do. I didn't realize that wherever He called me He would be with me and we would have a wonderful life. I have finally learned that there is no one who can compare to Jesus. No one who loves me as He loves me or is more concerned about me. Now I know I can safely put my life in His hands and He will do what is best for me.

Thank you, Lord for giving me Glen, a loving and patient husband for nearly 65 years. He was the love of my life. Clean in body and mind, with a sensitive nature, that when wounded was slow to heal. He was smarter, wiser, with more potential than he ever knew, and he suffered internally because he felt he did not measure up to others. And he was gentle and slow to speak and never spoke evil of anyone in our whole life together. Glen was faithful to the Lord and to the church, and he hardly ever missed in attendance or in giving his tithe offering to the Lord. And when there were other special needs, he quickly responded. I was so fortunate to have been his wife for all those years. I wish I could whisper in his ear one more time that I love him.

Thank you Lord for giving us three beautiful girls, when we thought we would never have a family. Each one was a miracle, being born two months premature and all living without extra life saving support. Each girl is so very different, yet so very much alike. When they call me on the phone I have to ask who's calling, because they sound the same. Being different, they show their love in different ways. They married strong husbands who are just right for them and their husbands have given them good Christian homes, with loving and happy families.

Thank you, Lord for every one of my grandchildren. Six by birth and two more by marriage, and still counting, four girls and four boys. What a miracle they are. How proud I am of them all and how fortunate I am that I can look with joy at them and know that God gave them to us. And now I have been blessed with a great-granddaughter Madelyn Lou, who is truly a little darling. I pray I'll live to see her grow and develop into the lovely young lady God designed her to be.

This road of life has been a long road. It has taken me a long time to know Him and His purpose for my life. For so much of the time I was a dreamer, who sought a place on a stump by a creek or in a cherry tree behind our house. It took years for me to realize God wanted me to follow the shepherd in loving obedience, instead of being the leader who was in charge.

Ephesians 2:8-10 "For it is by grace you have been saved, through faith and this not from yourselves, it is the gift of God not by works, so that no one can boast. For we are God's workmanship, created in Christ Jesus to do good works, which God prepared in advance for us to do."

It is by God's superior mercy, that my debt for sins committed has been paid for, by Jesus' death on the cross. Nothing that I could have done would have been able to pay the debt I owed, or I would be boasting to others. Since that first feeble step toward Him, He has been crafting my life to be more like Him and preparing me ahead of time to do for Him what He wanted me to do. Like a finish carpenter He took my life, a rough piece of humanity and carefully carved it into the door, that only I can open for Him to enter to accomplish what was destined in advance for me to do.

> *"Here I am. I stand at the door and knock. If anyone hears my voice and opens the door, I will come in and eat with him, and he with me."*
>
> Rev 3:20

I have enjoyed His presence through all the seasons of my life; childhood, teenager, young adult, newlywed, mother, grandmother, widow, great-grandmother and now short timer. How long He will allow me to follow Him here on this earth I don't know. But I intend to practice His presence with joy and show forth His love, by faithfully loving and praying for my family and others, and hopefully leading them closer to the Savior.

Acknowledgements

Two years ago when I began to write "Show Me The Way To Go Home." I had no idea where to start. Encouragement from family and friends along with their faith that I could do it was the catalyst I needed to begin. There were some however, who served way above the line of duty and I want to mention them individually.

Gloria Verdino, my dear friend from New York City, was with me first and helped wherever I needed it most. Way to go Gloria, I thank you for all your help.

And then long time friend Joy Harrison took on the gigantic job of editing the manuscript and stayed with me in the complicated process of submission to the publishers. Thanks Joy, you are a Godsend and I love you.

I could not fail to mention my son-in-law Bill Morris who has responded to my computer needs and helped me when I'd mess things up. Thank you Bill, you have helped me so very much.

And then special thanks to all you prayer warriors who prayed for me when I was sick and discouraged and felt I could not continue. The Lord answered your prayers and restored my health, sharpening my mind and helping me to finish the task.

To my little friend Mitzi who patiently slept under my chair while I labored away at the computer. There was a time when I had an apartment on the 2nd floor of Crista Shores and dogs were not allowed there. My close friend Lee Mae Elkins and her family took good care of Mitzi for me as I waited a year for an apartment to vacate on the beach level where dogs were allowed. Lee Mae you are a real friend and Mitzi will be yours someday when I can no longer care for her.

Thank you Lord for not giving up on me. Even though I was disobedient to your call, you loved me and showered me with your blessings. This story I have written to glorify you and to let my readers know that You alone know the way home.